Wild
AWAKENING

Wild

AWAKENING

How a Raging Grizzly
Healed My Wounded Heart

GREG J. MATTHEWS

with JAMES LUND

HOWARD BOOKS
NEW YORK   LONDON   TORONTO   SYDNEY   NEW DELHI

HOWARD BOOKS

Howard Books
An Imprint of Simon & Schuster, Inc.
1230 Avenue of the Americas
New York, NY 10020

First Howard Books hardcover edition June 2019

HOWARD and colophon are trademarks of Simon & Schuster, Inc.

For information about special discounts for bulk purchases, please contact Simon & Schuster Special Sales at 1-866-506-1949 or business@simonandschuster.com.

The Simon & Schuster Speakers Bureau can bring authors to your live event. For more information or to book an event, contact the Simon & Schuster Speakers Bureau at 1-866-248-3049 or visit our website at www.simonspeakers.com.

Manufactured in the United States of America

10 9 8 7 6 5 4 3 2 1

Library of Congress Cataloging-in-Publication Data has been applied for.

ISBN 978-1-5011-9453-5
ISBN 978-1-5011-9455-9 (ebook)

Dedicated to you, Dad, my best friend;
my brother, Matt, the hero;
and my anchors: my wife, Rhea, and my kids Casey, Benjamin,
and Ciara, who gave me the strength to survive.

CONTENTS

PROLOGUE

Razor-sharp fangs plunge into my side and lift me four feet into the air. The pain is excruciating. I'm slammed onto the ground, but those daggers don't loosen their grip. I am dragged over dead limbs, leaves, dirt. My fingers dig trenches in the soil, but my efforts fail to halt our deadly progress. A river of red fills one of the furrows in the dirt behind me. It's blood—my blood.

I am at the mercy of a monster.

Where is this thing taking me? I'm sliding into the abyss of irreversible shock. I've lost my voice. My strength to fight is all but gone. I think of my wife, Rhea, and my kids, Casey, Ben, and Ciara.

Then I think of God, the one I've entrusted with my life, the one who has always come through for me. Until now.

Lord, how could you let this happen? I want to see my family again. Please make it stop!

Suddenly I am released. Where is it? Using up what little reserve I have left, I lift my head.

Mere inches away, angry, coal-black eyes stare into mine. Hot, foul-smelling breath washes over me. My ears fill with the sound of a low, rumbling growl.

For just an instant, I catch the glint of white fangs as they lunge for my throat.

With a jerk of terror, I sit up. I'm in a bed, gasping for air, covered in sweat. Darkness surrounds me.

Where am I? Is this a nightmare or is it real?

What is happening to me?

SON SHINE AND STORM

They say that abandonment is a wound that never heals. I say
only that an abandoned child never forgets.
—MARIO BALOTELLI

I took a few stealthy steps and stopped. With each breath, white puffs rose from my lips into the crisp morning air. Ahead of me, stretching to rolling hills in the distance, was a mostly desolate landscape dotted with sagebrush, cactus, and sand as far as the eye could see. I was in the sprawling Mojave Desert. My grip tightened on the rifle in my hands and I slowly turned my head, straining my eyes for the slightest sign of movement. I was on safari, a mighty hunter at last.

It was December 27, 1974. I was nearly eight years old. My weapon was a brand-new Marlin .22. My quarry was the mighty jackrabbit.

I trembled with excitement. How many hours on how many nights had I lain in the upper berth of my bunk bed at home, staring at the posters of deer and bears I'd put up on my wall, imagining this day? Yet the best part wasn't being in the outdoors or the anticipation of hunting game for the first time, though each of these was a prize in itself. Nope, the real reward was sharing this moment with the broad-shouldered man who stood next to me.

Dad.

Roger Matthews, son of a World War II air force veteran, was a former Marine infantryman who these days wore the beige uniform of a California Highway Patrol officer. He was an imposing figure: six-foot-one, with an athletic build, a military haircut, and gray eyes that often seemed to bore through you. In many ways, he led his family—my mom, Elizabeth, and my younger brothers, Shane, age six, and Matt, age three—the way a sergeant might lead his platoon. When Dad told you to do something, there was no discussion or negotiation, and you'd better be getting started by the time he finished telling you. You addressed his friends and acquaintances as "sir." If you weren't fifteen minutes early, you were late. Good manners were required at all times. Dad wasn't mean and we weren't in boot camp, but the sense of military structure was undeniable.

To me, this was simply who my father was. His disciplined approach to life and our family made perfect sense to him and to me. It was one of the things that enabled him to do a dangerous job. Each time my father walked out of the house in the morning, that seven-point gold badge on his chest and pistol holstered at his side, I nearly burst with pride. He was a man who could handle himself, a man who took on the bad guys each day and won, a man people could count on.

He was my hero. I wanted to be just like him.

By the time of our rabbit hunt in the desert, Dad had spent three years teaching me gun safety, how to aim, and how to clean a rifle.

I'd already joined him on many hunts for quail and jackrabbits. Some days he'd pick me up early from kindergarten in his bright red Ford Bronco, drive out to a ravine on the back side of Big Bear Lake, and set up beside some boulders. My job was spotter and retriever. When I saw a flight of doves coming into range, I alerted Dad, who shot the birds out of the sky. I then ran into the bush to retrieve the doves and drop them into a hunting vest. We'd do that until dark. I was more like the hunting dog than the hunter, but I didn't mind. I loved those outings, just Dad and me and the great outdoors.

Sometime during the last few months, I'd decided I was old enough to hunt with Dad using a rifle of my own. Every Saturday that fall, I walked to the local library and pored over the latest editions of *Field & Stream*, *Outdoor Life*, and *Sports Afield* magazines. I was searching for my weapon of choice—a Marlin .22 semiautomatic with a clip. I thought if I found one on sale, it would be easier to convince Dad to buy me one for Christmas.

I'd already made my wishes known. My Christmas list had only two items: the Marlin rifle and a box of ammo. I'd set my heart on getting that rifle. I was like Ralphie, the boy who longed for a Red Ryder BB gun in the movie *A Christmas Story*. I'm amazed no one told me I'd shoot my eye out.

But Dad never gave me the slightest hint that he was thinking about it. Whenever I brought it up, he'd say, "Well, I'm not sure about that yet." By Christmas Eve I'd pretty much resigned myself to disappointment—it seemed the Marlin was not in my future. I tossed and turned in my bed that night. The numbers on the digital clock on my nightstand seemed frozen in place. I finally fell asleep at 2 a.m., then woke up three hours later. Fearing the worst but no longer able to contain myself, I crept down the dark hallway and into a room shimmering with Christmas magic.

My eyes first took in the five stockings tacked to the fireplace mantel, the material stretched and bulging from goodies hidden inside. Below, a gas fire was already glowing. Then I swept my gaze to the left and saw our Christmas tree, which was decorated with shining multicolored lights and surrounded by a mountain of presents. I quickly scanned the pile of packages. I knew the shape I was looking for—only it wasn't there.

But when I stepped forward and looked behind the tree, I saw it. A long, slender box leaned against the wall. Could it be? I hurried over to inspect the tag. It read: "From Santa." But who was it for?

This has to be it, I thought. *But what if it's not? It must be mine. But maybe it isn't.* My emotions bounced back and forth like a Ping-Pong ball.

Every year, Dad insisted that we kids open our biggest Christmas presents last. After everyone got up, I unwrapped a dozen packages, but my eyes never strayed long from that tall present. Finally, Dad grinned and said the words I'd been waiting to hear: "Greg, that box against the wall is for you." I tore off the paper and found exactly what I'd dreamed of. In the reflection of the Christmas tree lights, the Marlin rifle's barrel glinted like gold.

Dad had come through.

Now, two days later, I was finally in the desert with my father, ready to test my hunting skills against whatever nature had to offer. My legs shook with anticipation. We stood side by side, each of us scanning the terrain ahead. Suddenly, from the corner of my right eye, I caught a flash of movement. A jackrabbit!

"Dad!" I yelled. I pulled the Marlin's stock to my shoulder.

But the crafty jackrabbit had accelerated to Mach 2 and was already fifty yards away. I had no chance at a shot. Then I realized it wouldn't have mattered anyway—I'd forgotten to flip the rifle's safety off.

"Hold on, Greg," Dad said in a quiet voice. "You'll get your chance at him." Then he explained the secret of rabbit hunting: "They always run in a circle to get behind the threat that's chasing them. If we turn 180 degrees and start walking back, we'll run into him again."

That's just what we did, with Dad in the lead. And he was right. Not a hundred yards from where we'd started, Dad raised his hand and signaled me forward. Now I was really shaking. I drew up close to Dad and sighted along his outstretched arm. Twenty-five yards away, I saw the silhouette of ears through a clump of sagebrush.

Dad nudged me forward. "There he is, Greg, your first rabbit," he whispered. "Remember, just squeeze the trigger."

Slowly, I raised the Marlin and flipped off the safety. I felt my heart pound. It seemed as if the rifle barrel bounced with each beat. I aligned the front pin with the rear site. The barrel was aimed above my target, so I gently lowered it. I realized I was holding my breath. "Breathe, Greg," I muttered.

The site settled just behind the rabbit's left front leg. As I held the rifle's position, it felt as if it weighed a hundred pounds. Almost imperceptibly, my finger put pressure on the trigger. This was it, years of hopes and dreams caught up in this one moment with my dad.

The blast of the rifle surprised me. The recoil struck my shoulder. I realized I'd shut my eyes.

Dad's voice pierced the air: "You got him, Greg. You got him!"

I ran as fast as that rabbit had to where I knew I'd find him. My yell of delight roared across the desert.

Dad arrived and put his arm around me. "Congratulations, Greg," he said. "You're a real hunter now." The approval in Dad's eyes made it the proudest moment of my young life.

* * *

IF YOU WERE A YOUNG boy and got to pick where you would grow up, you'd have a hard time making a better choice than sunny San Diego. We lived in the Mira Mesa area at the northern edge of the city. Every day, it seemed, a new adventure beckoned. Shane and I often got up at 4 a.m., grabbed our tackle boxes, taped our fishing rods to our bikes, and rode five miles to Miramar Lake to catch rainbow trout, bluegill, catfish, or largemouth bass. Closer to home was the canyon—really just a large gully—with a creek. Almost every day after school, Shane and I took off our shoes and caught crawdads, built forts, and played war in our neighborhood wilderness. Sometimes we included three-year-old Matt, if we were tasked with babysitting duty.

My mother, a stay-at-home mom, was in many ways everything Dad was not. While Dad struggled with being affectionate, Mom loved to give her boys hugs, taught us how to say "I love you," and was so attentive when she talked with us that you couldn't help feeling you were special. Dad's ever-changing schedule didn't always allow him to be there for our games and school activities, but we could count on Mom being there.

Since we didn't see Dad as often, the times we did have with him were especially meaningful. The best of those were always somewhere in the open air. Dad wasn't an expert hunter or fisherman, but he loved the outdoors nonetheless. He felt he'd been born in the wrong century. He believed he was meant to be a mountain man who hunted, fished, and lived off the land. Every summer, Dad took us boys to the Sierra Nevada Mountains for a week of camping, exploring, and reeling in hundreds of trout from icy streams. Fishing poles, tents, BB guns, and campfires were our world. The fish we caught and the game we killed were treated respectfully—an animal had died so we could eat, therefore nothing was wasted. Those times in the wild with Dad—in fact, the first eight years of my life—were like a wonderful dream.

Sports were another opportunity to spend time with Dad. He didn't talk much about having been an athlete when he was younger, but he loved seeing me and my brothers excel on the playing fields. I was six years old when I first threw a baseball. A friend of Dad's saw me reach back and hurl that thing and said I was a natural, so Dad started catching me in the backyard. After I turned seven, I played Little League baseball in the spring, summer, and winter. I wasn't bigger than other kids my age, but I already had broad shoulders and was strong. I guess I *was* a natural—I had enough success both as a pitcher and hitter that other coaches started showing up at my games to scout me for their teams in the future.

I knew Dad was proud of me. He reveled in every strikeout and home run. Hugs, kisses, and comforting words were not part of his arsenal, but when I performed well, he bragged about me to friends with a twinkle in his eye. There was a dark side, however, to my athletic achievements and Dad's praise. Maybe Mom's unqualified support made me desire Dad's approval even more. Maybe it was simply that every young boy wants his father to be proud of him. Whatever the reason, I wanted to please him so badly that I put enormous pressure on myself. I began suffering from headaches and an upset stomach before games. I was afraid of failing. I did not want to let Dad down.

The other dark cloud in my life was the occasional fights between my parents, which seemed to increase as I got older. They seemed to happen only after my brothers and I went to bed. Sometimes the yelling got so loud that I just put my pillow over my head. One night, Mom was screaming at Dad. Then I heard the sound of glass shattering. In the morning, a trail of broken plates littered the floor from the kitchen into the dining room.

As bad as those fights were, everything always seemed to quickly return to normal. Mom and Dad acted as if nothing was wrong, so I didn't worry about it. I figured the yelling and fighting were just part of ordinary family life.

That was still my attitude on a hot day about seven months after I received the Marlin .22. It was the summer before I would enter fifth grade. My brothers and I were playing Wiffle ball in our front yard. Dad, wearing a polo shirt, jeans, and tennis shoes, emerged from the front door of our home carrying a couple of boxes. He walked to his beige Chevy Malibu parked in the driveway, set the boxes in the backseat, and headed back toward the house.

"What are you doing, Dad?" I asked before he reached the door.

"Just carrying some boxes."

"Can we help?" my brothers and I said in unison. Dad didn't answer. He just kept walking toward the house. Shane, Matt, and I ran to catch up and filed into the house behind him. We found a pile of boxes stacked in our parents' bedroom. Now it was a competition between us boys to see who could help Dad the most. We raced back and forth with boxes, loading the back seat of the car until you couldn't even see out the back window.

Once all but two of the boxes had been moved, we stood on the sidewalk next to the Chevy with ear-to-ear grins and waited for Dad's words of praise. Who would he say was the best helper? Shane and Matt argued about who carried the most boxes and who helped Dad the most. My father walked across the lawn carrying the final boxes. Without a word, he placed them in the front passenger seat of the Chevy. He didn't look at us. He *couldn't* look at us.

Dad walked around the front of the car, opened the driver's-side door, and just stood there. We looked at him and wondered what was going on. "Dad," I asked, "what are all the boxes for?"

He dropped his head, then finally looked each of us in the eye. "Boys, your mother and I still love each other, and this has nothing to do with you, but I'm not going to be living here anymore. I promise that we will see each other."

What?

I was in shock. This wasn't possible. Tears began streaming down my face. Suddenly, my whole world was disintegrating in front of me. Both of my brothers were now sobbing. In a pleading voice, Shane cried out, "Dad, please don't go."

Dad dropped his head again. "I have to go, boys." He got into the Chevy, shut the door, and drove away without looking back.

My life would never be the same again.

2

ON TO ALASKA

Delight yourself in the Lord, and he will give you the desires of
your heart.
—PSALM 37:4 ESV

6:30 A.M., TUESDAY, SEPTEMBER 15
DALLAS, TEXAS

In terms of landings and takeoffs, Dallas/Fort Worth International Airport was the third busiest airfield in the world. On an early September morning in 2015, commuters with briefcases and roll-away luggage were already herding into the terminal when my wife, Rhea, and I pulled up to the curb at the departures area. I didn't mind the crowd of travelers one bit, however. I couldn't wait to join them.

I jumped out of our Chevy Silverado 4x4, slipped on my travel back-pack, and walked to the back of the pickup. I unloaded an expeditionary bag and a Marine duffel bag onto the sidewalk, both of them waterproof and neatly packed with hunting and camping gear, clothing, and critical equipment. Next to the dry bags I placed the most beautiful rifle/bow hard case on the planet. I'd carved out most of the interior foam padding to fit five thousand dollars' worth of hunting and survival gear: binoculars, GPS, knives, revolver, clips, arrows, a Thompson/Center Venture bolt-action rifle, and a Mathews No Cam compound bow.

I was ready.

Rhea had gotten out of the car and stood a few feet away with her arms crossed. My wife is the kind of person everybody loves to confide in. She has a magnetic personality—warm, inviting, and sincere. When she turns on her megawatt smile, it lights up a room. In that moment at the airport, however, the huge smile I loved so much was missing.

"Are you going to be okay?" I asked.

"Oh, yeah, we'll be fine," Rhea said. "We'll be praying for you."

I stepped forward, squeezed my wife tight, and gave her a kiss. "I love you," I said.

"I love you too. Go chase your dream."

I grinned. "I'm so excited."

"I know you are. Just be careful. Please."

I grabbed my gear and stepped toward the sliding double doors that led into the terminal. Just before entering, I turned. Cars had lined up behind the Chevy, so Rhea was already pulling away. "I love you, sweetie," I said under my breath. Even though she wasn't looking, I blew her a last kiss. Then I walked into the terminal and headed for the gate. I could swear my feet weren't even touching the ground. The moment I'd been waiting for had finally come. I was headed to the Alaskan wilderness.

My love for hunting had not wavered since that day I shot my first jackrabbit with Dad in the Mojave Desert. I'd hunted deer, pigs, and coyotes for years, but I had never had the opportunity to pursue one of the largest game mammals in the Americas: an Alaskan moose. A male might stand seven feet tall at the shoulders, weigh over fourteen hundred pounds, and sport antlers that spanned six feet. Hunting this regal denizen of the wild was definitely one of my dreams, but as was the case for so many who'd discovered the price of a guided moose hunt in Alaska, my dream had seemed destined to remain just that.

Then, two years before, I'd received a phone call from Matt. My baby brother had served his country in the air force for twenty years, including a deployment and additional duty in Iraq. His final duty assignment was at Joint Base Elmendorf-Richardson in Anchorage. He'd retired from the air force and become a government contractor; he and his family were Alaska residents.

Like me, Matt was an avid hunter. He'd shot caribou and moose in the wilds of his adopted state. He knew how badly I wanted to hunt a moose myself. Now he had an idea.

"Greg, I think you and Shane and I need to go on a bull moose hunt up here," he said. "I've already started planning. We can load up a river jet boat for a ten-day hunt into the interior. I already know the type of boat I want to buy. We can take a year to plan everything and then go the following season. What do you think? Do you want to head out for a big-game hunt and Alaskan adventure?" Matt paused for a split second. "Greg, I want the Matthews brothers to face the wilds of Alaska and test what kind of men we really are."

With every word, I'd grown more excited. By the time Matt finished speaking and asked for my opinion, I was nearly speechless. I should have talked to Rhea about it first. I should have considered the financial implications. But in that moment I only wanted to respond before Matt could change his mind.

"Yes," I nearly shouted. "Yes, I'm in!"

Fortunately, once I explained Matt's idea to my understanding wife, she gave it her blessing and support. I immediately dove into preparations.

You might say that I am fairly intense about whatever I commit to. My family and friends would go further—they'd probably accuse me of having obsessive-compulsive disorder. I do like to be prepared for anything. Rhea still teases me about it. Even if my objective is only to take a shower, she says I'll still have a plan A and a plan B. (In case you're wondering, in a pinch, a warm washcloth can substitute for a shower just fine.)

Now I had a new project to focus on. I spent all my free hours planning for every aspect of the trip: hunting techniques, navigation, communications, maps, equipment, water purification, food, transportation, licenses and tags, fuel management, first aid, physical conditioning, tents, kitchen setup, sleeping, hauling out the game, cleaning and field dressing, survival techniques, and emergency preparations. I made dozens of pages of notes in a journal, which included a list of every piece of gear I would bring to Alaska and how to operate and power it. Every night when I went to bed, the upcoming adventure was all I could think about.

I purchased the Thompson/Center Venture rifle, as fine a weapon as I'd ever owned. It was matte gray, with a nylon slip-resistant stock, and used .300 Winchester Magnum ammunition. I outfitted that with a top-of-the-line, 4-16x42 Nikon Monarch BDC scope, which was deadly out to five hundred yards. I lived in San Diego at the time, so for practice, I hunted javelina and feral hogs in the mountainous terrain of Vandenberg Air Force Base on California's central coast, as well as hogs, quail, doves, and rabbits in the desert region near El Centro, close to the border with Mexico. I needed to raise my hunting skills to the highest possible level.

Another important part of my preparation was studying what to do if the Matthews brothers somehow became the prey during our hunt. The possibility seemed unlikely, but I planned to leave nothing to chance. My focus was on two potential predators. The first was the wolf. Wolf attacks in Alaska were infrequent, but they did occur. In 2010, a schoolteacher was fatally mauled by at least two wolves near Chignik Lake.

Wolves traveled in packs and could appear suddenly and silently. The plan was to always be on high alert, with one eye on what we were doing and the other on our surroundings. We would not be defenseless. In addition to carrying my rifle and bow, I would holster a .357 Magnum revolver and sheath a ten-inch KA-BAR knife on my hip at all times. Our best protection against a pack of wolves, however, would be a 12-gauge tactical shotgun loaded to fire eight rounds of three-inch Magnum slugs and buckshot. In a close-quarters encounter, our shotgun would discourage a host of unwelcome guests in a hurry.

It was less likely that we would face the other predator on our list, though this one was even more dangerous. In Alaska, the king of the food chain was the North American brown bear, *Ursus arctos horribilis*, better known as the grizzly bear.

A grizzly might weigh as much as 850 pounds, stand eight and a half feet on its hind legs, and run as fast as thirty-five miles per hour. It has a better sense of smell than a bloodhound and can sniff out food three miles away. What really gives any woodsman pause, however, is the grizzly's powerful claws and jaw. With a single swipe of its paw, which includes nails up to six inches long, the grizzly can kill an animal as large as a moose. The brown bear's jaw, meanwhile, contains fangs that range up to four inches in length. The force of a grizzly's bite has been measured at more than eleven hundred pounds per square inch—enough to crush a bowling ball.

To make matters worse, the grizzly is more aggressive than its cousin, the black bear. It is more prone to defending itself, particularly when the grizzly in question is a mama protecting her cubs. Environmentalist Timothy Treadwell and his girlfriend, Amie Huguenard, were killed and partly devoured by a grizzly in October 2003 after they camped close to a salmon stream in Alaska's Katmai National Park.

Grizzlies were more apt than wolves to avoid people, however, and more likely to go another way if they heard human conversation. If any animal would threaten us during our hunt, I was sure it would be a wolf. Either way, I felt prepared for whatever nature had to throw our way.

I soon learned that I wasn't the only one thinking about predators. One night when I was in my home office, Rhea appeared in the doorway and leaned against the frame. I was in the middle of tracing the contours of my revolver onto the foam padding of the weapons case. When I cut out the foam, the gun would have a snug resting place during the trip.

My wife glanced at the room and all my packed equipment. "Wow," she said, "that's a lot of gear." She noticed the .357 Magnum resting on the weapons case and nodded toward it. "Where did you get that one?"

I finished tracing, then almost reverently picked up the revolver. "This is one of the first handguns Dad ever gave me," I said. "It's the same type of pistol that he carried on the highway patrol." I pointed out the image of a highway patrol star located just behind the cylinder on the revolver. "This is what I'm going to carry on my hip for extra protection against bears." As I held it in my hands, I thought about the fact that my dad had defended his life as a law enforcement officer by carrying this same weapon. If Dad could trust it, I certainly could.

Rhea's brow furrowed. "Are you worried about running into a bear?"

"No," I said. "Just in case, we've done a lot of preparation for a possible encounter. But I'm really not concerned about it. Although the one thing I do need to buy after we get up there is some bear spray."

Now Rhea looked puzzled.

"Bear spray?" she said. "Is that like mosquito repellent? Do you spray it all over your clothes or something?"

I couldn't help laughing. "No, silly, you spray it at the bear's face and nose. It chases him away, or at least that's what the magazines say. The only thing spraying it on my clothes would do is season me like a steak."

We both laughed this time. I explained that bears have an especially acute sense of smell and would not care one bit for having the unpleasant odor of cayenne pepper sprayed in their face.

"Does it work?" Rhea asked.

"According to the advertisements it does. I've never had the joy of testing it. But it's another layer of protection."

Rhea, still leaning against the doorjamb, crossed her arms. She didn't look convinced that we would be safe, so I made another try at reassuring her.

"Matt lives up there and knows the territory," I said. "We have done a ton of preparation. Everything's going to be fine. You don't have anything to worry about."

AFTER A YEAR OF INTENSE planning for the Alaska trip and only six weeks before I was supposed to leave, I realized I had to make a heartrending phone call. I'd been putting in long hours at my job

in San Diego. Rhea and the kids needed more from me as a husband and a dad. So that I could spend more time with my family, we
decided that I would accept a job in Plano, Texas. It would be a new
start, with less of a demand on my time and attention. The problem
was that my first day at work in fall 2014 was only two weeks before
our scheduled adventure in Alaska. Shane had already reluctantly
dropped out of the hunt. He had diabetes and feared that he would
slow us down. Now I was delivering more bad news to Matt.

I hemmed and hawed before finally explaining about the move
and my new job. "I have done everything in my power to try to
realign the timing of this change," I said. "But I need to commit to
this job. This is a big, big decision for my family. There's not much
that would stand in the way of me being there with you, but this is
one of those things."

Fortunately, Matt was amazingly gracious. "You know what?" he said.
"That's okay. It'll give me more time for preparation and to get things set
here. I understand. I've had to make decisions for my family that impacted
other things. We'll just plan on going the same time next year."

Despite my brother's kind words, I was deeply disappointed. I
slipped into an emotional funk. To salve the wounds of this setback,
I increased the intensity of my preparations. I reinventoried my gear,
reread my journal notes, and refined my supplies. I also made an
important decision—I would hunt the Alaskan moose with a compound bow.

I'd always enjoyed the challenge of leveling the playing field
between hunter and hunted. It forced me to be more cunning, silent,
and stealthy in order to get in position for a shot. I had to learn to
blend in, use the wind to my advantage, and understand where my
quarry migrated, where they fed, and where they bedded down. For
me, hunting wasn't about the kill but about the one-on-one pursuit.

If I took on the Alaskan moose with bow and arrow, it would multiply both the challenge and the satisfaction if I succeeded.

Not long after arriving in Texas, I began spending hours every day in our backyard shooting arrows at targets the size of a baseball. I also found the perfect opponent for refining my skills. The Texas boar, also known as a Russian wild boar, is smart, with a nose more sensitive than a bloodhound's and ears that can hear a snapping twig over a quarter mile away. A wounded hog with sharp tusks is dangerous, so when I hunted these wily creatures I had to combine stealth with an accurate shot. During multiple hunts in that second year of preparation I actually killed only two boars. Each time I drew back my bow, I imagined it was the one and only shot I would ever get at a moose. I often held my bow drawn on a boar for minutes at a time in order to help me learn to control my breathing.

Back at the Dallas/Fort Worth airport, as I settled into my seat on the plane, I thought about those endless hours of preparation. *It's finally happening. I'm going to Alaska!*

After I'd fastened my seat belt, another memory filled my mind, one both heartwarming and bittersweet. My oldest son, Casey, was away at college, but my two younger children—Ben, age eleven, and Ciara, almost nine—were still at home. Since I'd needed to get up so early in the morning to make my flight, I'd said my goodbyes the night before.

I had stacked all my gear near our entryway, then asked Rhea to send in the kids. They'd been doing their homework. Since it was almost their bedtime, they were in their pajamas, Ben wearing a T-shirt and flannel bottoms and Ciara in all flannel. Both had questioning looks on their faces.

"Hey," I said, "I'm going to be leaving really, really early in the morning for my Alaska trip, so I'm not going to wake you up. I just want to tell you that I love you and get my hugs and kisses tonight."

Both kids came over, Ciara on the left and Ben on my right, and placed their heads against my chest. I put one arm around each of them. Then Rhea joined in behind them, wrapping her arms around all of us. We tried to squeeze the air out of one another. Since I'd missed that with my dad, I made a conscious effort never to hold back affection from my kids.

I gave Ciara a big kiss, then grabbed Ben, held him tight so he couldn't wriggle away, and kissed him on the neck about ten times.

"I love you, Daddy," Ciara said. "Please be careful out there."

I took in the image of my family—Ciara, concerned, and Ben, reveling in his dad's hugs and kisses, both looking up at me, and Rhea, enjoying this special moment—until it was burned into my consciousness. I would never forget the love in their eyes.

"I promise I'll be careful," I said. "We've been planning this for a long time, so we're ready. Daddy will be just fine."

I was so excited to start my adventure, but I would miss these three in my arms more than they would know. I was also concerned about leaving them on their own for two weeks. I was their protector. Once Matt and I reached the Alaskan wilderness, we wouldn't have cell phone service. I'd never been out of contact with my family for so long. As I held them close, I prayed silently for God to take care of each of them.

On the plane, my concerns quickly receded to the back of my mind. The hunt and my pursuit of a long-held dream were finally in reach. I couldn't wait to get started. I had no idea, of course, that it wasn't my family I should have been worried about. Or that my survival would soon depend on my memory of that snapshot in time, the life-giving image of my wife and children, their arms wrapped around me in an unbreakable embrace.

3

SUMMER DREAMS

*All in all, it was a never-to-be-forgotten summer—one of those
summers which come seldom into any life, but leave a rich
heritage of beautiful memories in their going.*
—L. M. MONTGOMERY

I knew what was coming.

For two weeks, more than a dozen eighth-grade boys had lined
both sides of a hallway that lower-grade students had to pass through
to get to their lockers and classes at Pepper Drive Elementary in El
Cajon, California. For the younger, smaller students, it was like running a gauntlet. As they moved past, the eighth-graders slapped at
their heads, spun books and yellow Pee-Chee folders out of their
hands, and taunted them. It was an all-too-common exercise in adolescent humiliation.

I knew all this because, in 1979, I was a seventh-grader at Pepper
Drive. I was one of those younger students.

On this particular day in May, I had just finished geography class
and was walking up the concrete steps on our terraced campus with

my friends Craig, Wayne, and Jon. Our pace slowed as we neared the dreaded left turn. To get to our lockers and math class, we had to pass through the hallway of doom.

"Hey," Craig said, "maybe we could go around the other way."

"No," Wayne said, shaking his head. "Then we can't put our books in our lockers. We'd have to haul 'em everywhere."

We were at the top of the stairs. It was decision time.

"All right," I said, "let's do this. Let's just press on through."

Although I expected it, my heart still sank when I turned the corner and saw the eighth-graders back in their familiar rows, ready to disgrace us yet again. The leaders were Aaron, Steve, and Scott—big, athletic guys with long hair, each wearing a T-shirt and Levi's 501 jeans. It seemed to me that their eyes gleamed when they saw us. They were like predators taking measure of their prey.

I'd escaped unscathed my last few times through the line. I tried to be optimistic. *We have a bunch of guys going through at once. Maybe they'll leave us alone.* We plunged in. By ducking and dodging, I managed to avoid any blows. I saw I was near the end, Steve on the right, Aaron and Scott on the left. Scott wore a T-shirt with a lightning bolt across the front. I quickened my pace.

I thought I was going to make it, but I was so focused on the hands aiming attempted blows at my head that I missed what was going on at my feet. A leg was extended. I ran right into it, tripped, and fell as if in slow motion to my stomach. Pee-Chees, books, and my body slid across the concrete floor.

The eighth-graders hooted. One called out, "Don't you know how to walk?" That line drew laughs from the gang. My friends were silent.

I got to my knees and slowly started picking up my books and papers. What everyone in that hallway surely saw was a meek and humiliated seventh-grader. What they couldn't see was the fury build-ing inside me. I'd been angry that whole year—at what exactly, I didn't know. I'd beat up guys a couple times earlier, students who were pick-ing on my brother Shane. Dad had taught his sons how to defend themselves and one another. The Matthews boys would not be victims.

I didn't seek conflict, but I didn't avoid it either. And in that moment, I had reached my limit.

After I picked up my books and papers and got to my feet, I shuf-fled back down the line with my head down. The eighth-graders were still laughing. I'm sure they thought I was being submissive. But I was looking at shoes. During my inglorious fall, I'd caught a glimpse of the shoe on the leg that tripped me: a black Converse.

It didn't take long to find a pair of black Converse sneakers on the left side of the line. They were Scott's.

I glanced up. Scott grinned, revealing his braces. "Oh, I'm sorry," he said. "Didn't you see my leg out there?"

My balled fist hit Scott in the jaw before he could utter another word. He dropped to the floor faster than an elevator without a cable.

I didn't stick around to see how Scott was doing. I hurried off to math class. But I knew I was in trouble. It wasn't long before I was called out of class and into the office of Mr. Metz, formerly a profes-sional baseball player and now our principal. My punishment was ten home run swings with a paddle on my backside and a weeklong suspension.

Much worse, however, was seeing Dad.

When Dad left our family four years before, my brothers and I stayed with Mom. My parents divorced soon after. Dad paid child support, but Mom still couldn't afford to keep the house. We moved into a smaller home across the street. Mom did the best she could, working part-time as a dental assistant or tending bar, anything to bring in a few dollars. But we never had much. Dad lived in a series of apartments and started going out with Brenda, a highway patrol dispatcher and nurse. When Dad bought a house near Pepper Drive Elementary, he and Brenda moved into it.

The house was far nicer than the place where Mom and my brothers and I lived. He'd bought a ranch-style home with a beige stucco exterior and ample front and back yards. During the summer before my sixth-grade year, when my parents asked where I wanted to live, I decided to move in with Dad and Brenda. My brothers decided to come too. I still couldn't believe everything had fallen apart, that our family was split and I had to choose between parents. I was nowhere near ready to deal with the emotions swirling inside me.

On the day of the hallway fight, I wasn't ready to deal with Dad either. My father hated to be embarrassed. I knew he would be furious and disappointed in me. As I sat on a chair in the waiting area outside of Mr. Metz's office, I dreaded Dad's arrival. Soon enough, there he was, in his uniform, walking down the hall in my direction. One look at his face was all it took to confirm that he was not pleased. I dropped my head. Dad was the one who'd taught me to defend myself and to not be a victim. I wanted so much to make him proud of me, to show him that I had what it took to be a man like him. Unfortunately, the principal was convinced I was being a bully. That look of disappointment from Dad brought on a hurt and a feeling of failure that burrowed deep.

Dad met with Mr. Metz behind a closed door. A few minutes later, Dad emerged, still grim-faced. "I'll make sure to take care of this," he said to Mr. Metz. "This won't happen again."

I sat in the back of the car on the way home. Dad glanced at me in the rearview mirror as he drove. "This is getting to be a regular thing with you," he finally said.

I tried to explain what had happened. But when Dad asked if I was defending myself when I threw the punch, I had to admit that I wasn't. That was all he needed to hear.

"You've had other fights this year already," he said. "Now you're suspended. We need to do something about this. You've lost your summer. You're going to be restricted to your room."

I knew there would be no negotiating or further discussion. My sentence was final. As soon as the school year ended, I spent all my time in my room. The only exceptions were meals and yardwork.

That first week was horrible. I had no TV. I knew I faced a summer with no hunting, no fishing, no baseball, no exploring. I shared the room with my brothers, but they had the freedom to roam the house or to leave and play with friends. Since the room included bunk beds and the captain's bed I slept in, it left me little room to move. I was reduced to looking out the bedroom window at the street and watching my friends throw a football.

I was miserable and mad about everything. My whole world had fallen apart. I felt I'd lost everything that I enjoyed, that I was in jail. I thought, *I am done with this.*

So I hatched a plan.

One day when I was alone with Shane, I said, "I'm thinking about running away to the wilderness and living off the land." For better and worse, my brothers looked up to me. When I explained more details of my scheme to Shane, he was all for it.

"I'm going with you," he said.

Suddenly my summer had a purpose. Since this was in the days before the internet, Shane and I examined encyclopedias and maps to decide on a destination. Our choice was the mountainous area around Dixie, Idaho, a remote and unincorporated community in the center of the state. It offered wildlife, forest, and streams, everything we thought we needed to make it on our own. Shane jumped on his bike each week and pedaled to the library to bring back books about fishing, hunting, travel, woodlore, and survival in the outdoors. We pored over those books, absorbing every ounce of information we could. We read about how to build fires, treat water, smoke fish and game, survive eating roots and berries, and build a log cabin with a chimney. We recorded detailed notes in a journal we kept hidden. We made lists of the equipment we'd need to survive the trip and that first winter and began scrounging around the house for supplies. Even Matt joined in, though he'd only just finished second grade. We promised to come back and visit and made him promise not to say a word about our plans to Dad.

I realized that knowledge and a few supplies from home wouldn't be enough to sustain us. We needed more materials and transportation, and that took money. So we asked Dad if we could work around the house and yard to earn cash during my confinement. Since my dad believed that manual labor was good punishment, he quickly put us to work installing a sprinkler system and building a retaining wall. Little did he know that we were rat-holing every dime and quarter he gave us in our getaway fund. I wasn't allowed to use the phone, so Shane called the local Greyhound bus station and learned we needed ninety-nine dollars apiece for a one-way ticket to Dixie. That was going to take a lot of yardwork.

The plans that Shane and I made in my room were more than a pipe dream. We expected to make our wilderness adventure a reality. What I didn't realize until years later was that it was less the adventure itself than the vision of it that gave me hope and got me through that summer. Each day was a full-blown operation filled with reviewing lists of techniques, tactics, and supplies. Shane and I dreamed of hunting deer, elk, and bear, and of surviving by our wits. It gave me a release for all my frustration. I already loved the outdoors, but during that summer of intense planning my appreciation for the wilderness skyrocketed. So did my bond with my brothers. Though they weren't obligated to hang out with their grounded older brother, they spent hours nearly every day with me. It was a time I would never forget.

Though each day brought me a little closer to my brothers, it was a different story with my dad. To me, my punishment seemed over-the-top. I was frustrated and angry, but I knew there was no arguing with Dad. I dealt with it by trying to avoid him and by enduring my pain in silence. At dinnertime, my brothers, Dad, Brenda, and I all sat at the table together, but our conversation was surface and minimal. Dad certainly didn't ask how I was feeling, and I wasn't about to tell him. As soon as the meal was over, I went back to my room.

I was sure that I was a continual disappointment to my father. It seemed I could never measure up. The only solution I could come up with was to get free from all of it and run away.

Our plan was to continue preparations, keep saving money, and sneak off the following spring. Then school started and my restriction was finally lifted. I was still angry, but my newfound freedom made life a bit more bearable. I found my thoughts turning more and more to baseball, friends, and girls. The dream of disappearing in Idaho died a slow and quiet death. My desire to pursue adventure in the wild and live a life without depending on anyone, however, was only beginning to grow.

4

OMENS

2 P.M., TUESDAY, SEPTEMBER 15

ABOVE ANCHORAGE, ALASKA

The captain's voice boomed over the intercom, waking me from a light sleep: "Please fasten your seat belts. We are making our final descent into Anchorage."

When I peered out the window of our Boeing 767, the clouds parted and wild Alaska materialized below me. Although the skies were cloaked in gray, a sea of green forests, brilliant-white snow-capped mountains, and miles of blue oceans and crooked rivers stretched for as far as I could see. The vastness and majesty of Alaska never failed to captivate me.

I had been here before. In 2004, I brought my family up to visit Matt's clan for a vacation. We all had a great time. And in 2012, I joined Matt on a weeklong fishing trip on the Kenai River. On that visit, I hooked a fifty-pound king salmon that I brought all the way to the boat on a fly rod, though it was out of season for salmon, so we had to cut the line. Those were great memories. Now I was thrilled to be back in the "last frontier."

After disembarking the 767, I hurried toward the baggage claim. My worst nightmare was that some of my gear didn't make it on the plane. I stopped in mid-stride, however, at the sight of an enormous glass display case in the middle of the airport. Inside it was the biggest stuffed grizzly I had ever laid eyes on. The brown bear, standing on its hind legs, dwarfed the stuffed wolf that gazed up in apparent terror from the bear's feet. The grizzly was nearly twice as tall as I was. Its open jaws revealed huge and deadly fangs. Four-inch-long claws extended from its massive paws. Its bulk was supported by powerful haunches that looked like tree stumps. While alive, that thing must have weighed four or five times what I did.

I shook my head. *I would hate to meet anything in the woods as ferocious and terrifying as that.*

I was too pumped up to dwell on that grim thought for long, however. This monster had been someone else's problem. I moved past the grizzly and continued to the baggage claim, where my dry bags were the first off the carousel. It took only a few moments more to pick up my gun case at the claim counter. All my gear had arrived safely. I finally breathed a sigh of relief. This was surely a good sign.

I was barely out the terminal doors when Matt pulled up in a new deep-blue Ford F-250 king cab truck. He grabbed me for a hug and hoisted my gear into the back of the truck. We were on our way.

"I am so excited," I said. "You have no idea. I am finally on the ground in Alaska."

Matt laughed. "You're right, Greg, you made it. It's time for the Matthews brothers to take adventure head-on."

I started talking faster than a giddy schoolgirl. "So what else do we need to get? When's the boat going to be ready? When should we go food shopping?" I pulled out my supply list and we went over the details. I was on such a pre-hunt "high" that our ninety-minute drive felt more like ten.

Matt and his family had just moved into a big, beautiful new split-level home in a rural area of Wasilla, a town about forty miles northeast of Anchorage. Their house overlooked an eighteen-hole golf course. When we arrived, Matt's wife, Melinda, and the kids seemed as happy to see me as I was to see them. My brother had an amazing family. Logan, the oldest at twenty-one, was introverted, smart, and tough. Even in snow and freezing temperatures, he used to ride a bicycle to his job at a local market. Now he had a four-wheeler. I was sorry to miss Rhiannon, a studious and affectionate nineteen-year-old who was away at college in Atlanta. Gareth, fourteen, had a big heart and had just purchased a new Nerf gun so he and I could do battle. Ariel, eleven, had a sparkle in her eyes and was ready to dote on me. "Uncle Greg, do you need anything?" she asked. "Are you warm enough? Do you want me to bring you a blanket?" The baby of the family was Lorilli Allana, a six-year-old with a bright smile and questions of her own: "How long have you been my daddy's brother? How come my daddy is taller than you if he's your little brother?"

Melinda was the one who kept this impressive herd going. She had homeschooled all the kids, organizing their academic lessons as well as coordinating activities such as music and tap dancing lessons and cheer and tumbling practices. Since Matt's work as a government contractor took him away from home for two months at a time, she'd also served as the general contractor on their new house. Now that I had arrived, she began preparing a delicious dinner: black bear meat loaf, potatoes, and kale chips, with blackberry cobbler for dessert.

After our meal, Matt and I retired to deck chairs on his wraparound back porch. We needed some beer and burping time to regain our man cards. We each sampled some Copenhagen dip (I've since given up tobacco chew) and enjoyed the spectacular view. The September sun seemed to move horizontally rather than set, splaying shafts of yellow and orange through pockets of towering Douglas fir trees. Beyond the tall timber, manicured greens, and fairways awaited the next day's links players. We'd been sitting only a few minutes when I observed a bald eagle flying overhead. This was as close to paradise as just about anything I could imagine.

Matt flashed a satisfied grin. "After all these years, I've finally got you up here to experience a true wilderness adventure," he said. "I'm so glad this is finally coming together. The Matthews brothers are going to test themselves against Alaska."

"Well, you know how glad I am to be here," I said. "I can't wait for us to get out there."

We still had details to take care of, however. Matt had ordered a new motor for his boat. I had to buy a hunting license and bear spray. And of course, we needed to stock up on food. So we spent the next two days getting ready, as well as relaxing with Matt's family. I learned that all of the kids were huge *Star Wars* fans. On both of the next two nights, we all sat down with bowls of popcorn and watched one of the franchise's original movies. The kids knew every line.

During our preparations, I also practiced my moose calls. When Matt told me that they sometimes spotted moose on the golf course, I immediately took my mechanical call onto the back porch and tried to lure one in. I had to admit that my first efforts sounded more like a dying moose than anything else. Matt could make a great moose call just by cupping his hands around his mouth and using his voice. He tried to encourage me, but in the end Matt said, "Yeah, I'll do the first set of calls, just to make sure we get 'em going in the right direction, toward us."

My brother must have realized how impatient I would be during these last few days to start hunting. To scratch my itch, he'd planned for us to go grouse hunting, something I'd never tried. We set out on an early morning for a lake southeast of Wasilla. Matt wanted to make sure that hunting was still allowed, so we pulled into a driveway to talk to a man who owned land in the area. As we got out of the truck, a portly gentleman with a brown-and-gray beard, wearing a Carhartt jacket and jeans, walked in our direction.

The land owner soon confirmed that it was fine for us to hunt in the area. But he added a warning.

"You need to be careful," he said. "I noticed a sow black bear and cubs have been coming up through the woods here. So just be aware of that."

Those words got my attention. I'd never confronted a bear face-to-face, but now that I was in Alaska it was a real possibility. Getting between a mama bear and her cubs was about the most dangerous place a man could be. I definitely didn't want that to happen, especially since I was carrying only a shotgun armed with bird shot and my .357 Magnum revolver. Those would not be near enough to stop an angry she-bear.

I was quickly distracted from my concerns, however, by what happened next. As we talked in the driveway, I spotted movement in the woods about seventy yards away. I blinked to make sure that what I was viewing was real—it was a cow moose, her ears twitching, eating leaves off a tree. Then a baby calf emerged from the woods and joined her.

Man, I thought, *these animals are just waiting for me to start flinging arrows at 'em. It's all right here!*

I was more eager to hunt than ever. Thankfully, it wasn't long before Matt and I reached our destination and began winding our way on foot through a heavily wooded area. The sky was overcast and gray, but the stands of alders had already started changing to yellow and gold, creating a picturesque contrast to the greens of Douglas fir, spruce, and pine trees. We walked slowly, thirty feet apart, across a series of small hills and gullies. Both of us carried our shotguns.

I was used to wing shooting, where our presence would flush a bird from its hiding place into the air. Though I hadn't seen or heard a thing, Matt suddenly raised his weapon.

Boom!

"I got one!" he yelled.

Sure enough, we quickly found the body of a grouse not ten yards ahead. I was clearly a rookie when it came to this kind of hunt.

"What are you looking for?" I asked.

"Watch the branches of these trees," he said, pointing ahead and up at a group of pines. "You'll see a little bit of movement. They'll be hiding on these branches."

Matt's advice led to good fortune. In an hour of hunting, we both bagged two grouse. We did a field dressing on the grouse at the back of Matt's truck and made a tasty meal of them that evening.

I'd had a wonderful time with Matt's family. But after watching *The Empire Strikes Back* on the third night, it was time for final preparations and bed. Matt and I filled four thirty-gallon containers with gasoline for the boat and made sure everything was packed and ready. It was after twelve-thirty in the morning when I finally retired to Rhiannon's room. In just three and a half hours I would at last embark on the primary purpose of this trip—a moose-hunting adventure with my brother in the Alaskan wilderness.

I sat on the edge of the bed and glanced around. Stuffed animals patrolled the top of my niece's dresser, while pictures of Rhiannon and her friends performing gymnastics and cheer routines adorned the walls. The temperature was warm and the room was cozy. I knew that the next day's environment would be far different.

Was there anything else I needed to do? Had I forgotten anything? I realized that at this point, if I'd forgotten something, I would have to go without it. During two years of planning, I'd done everything possible to ensure the success of our hunt and our safety. Now everything seemed to be falling into place. I had all my gear, our preparations were complete, and all was well with my family and with Matt's. I'd even seen a moose already with my own eyes—if that wasn't a good omen, I didn't know what was.

Only two things could have made this moment more perfect. One was if Shane had been able to join us. I understood completely why Shane had decided to opt out. It just would have been extra special to have all three Matthews brothers together for this one.

The other missing piece, of course, was Dad.

5

SPIRAL

The loneliest moment in someone's life is when they are watching their whole world fall apart, and all they can do is stare blankly.
—F. SCOTT FITZGERALD

Not long after my parents divorced, my mom met a man named Gene while tending bar. They married in 1979, when I was twelve, but it was a relationship of convenience more than love. They split up soon after. A few months later, my mom met a painting contractor named Jeff and both of them fell hard for each other. My dad, meanwhile, was also moving on. I was fourteen when he married his live-in girlfriend, Brenda. Two years later, Mom married Jeff. If I'd had any hope of my parents getting back together and our family reuniting, that hope was now gone.

My parents seemed to be handling life a lot better than I was. I still lived with Dad and Brenda during my last year at Pepper Drive Elementary and my first year at El Cajon Valley High School. I continued to get into fights at both schools. I began hanging out with the older baseball and football players at El Cajon. To fit in, I started drinking beer, which only made things worse. Then came the time a few of my buddies and I decided to go to dollar movie night at the mall. While running around in the parking lot after the movie, we somehow decided that tearing down a stop sign was a good idea. Each of us took turns kicking and pulling until the sign finally lay dead in the street. We didn't notice until too late the headlights approaching at a swift pace. They belonged to a police squad car. It was my first arrest, but not my last.

You could say that my judgment was a bit questionable in those days. I was mad at the world and busy taking care of Greg. I didn't much care what anybody else thought.

By early spring of my sophomore year, I'd grown tired of the tension I felt around my dad and moved in with Mom and Jeff. As hard as I tried, I never felt I measured up to Dad's standards. It wasn't that his expectations were over-the-top. I just grew weary of attempting to be perfect for him.

One night a guy on the baseball team, Tony, drove me and another friend, James, over to a 7-Eleven, where we "fished" for beer—that is, we asked people going into the store if they'd buy us some. We eventually "caught" a case of beer and headed to Parkway Bowl, a combination of bowling alley, pool hall, and arcade. It was one of the local hangouts for the high school crowd.

The three of us alternated between the arcade and drinking beers in the car. James and I drank a few. By the end of two trips back and forth, Tony must have downed a twelve-pack.

After spending a couple hours inside Parkway, we decided it was time to head home. I noticed that Tony stumbled a bit on our walk to the car. Then he fumbled with his keys when he tried to unlock the door. Finally he staggered over to the passenger's-side front door, managed to open it, and dropped into the seat. A few seconds later he was puking on the floorboard.

James sat in the back seat and announced, "I'm not going to drive."

I had a curfew. I needed to get home.

I didn't have a driver's license, but my mom had let me practice a few times. It was mostly a straight shot to my house—a couple of intersections with traffic lights and one right turn onto my street. *I can do this*, I thought. *I can definitely do this.*

"Okay," I said. "I'll drive."

Tony's car was a Buick, big as a tuna boat. I did just fine backing up the Buick and maneuvering through the parking lot. What I didn't realize, however, was that I hadn't turned on the headlights. The lot was so well lit that I didn't notice.

I pulled onto the street and made it through the two traffic lights without a problem. Everything was going great. Then I missed the right turn to my street. I was in the process of turning around when a squad car's lights started flashing in my direction. A cop had noticed I was driving without headlights.

I knew I was in big trouble.

"Have you been drinking, son?" the officer asked.

"I've had a couple beers," I said.

"Are you legally old enough to drink?"

I realized there was no way out of this one. "No," I said.

The officer had me get out of the car and try to walk in a straight line. I couldn't do it. Then he had me blow into a Breathalyzer. Before I knew what was happening, he was putting cuffs on me and directing me into the back of his patrol car. I was being arrested for driving under the influence and driving without a license.

Dad hated drunk drivers. He'd seen them destroy the lives of too many innocent people. "It's the drunk drivers that always live," I'd heard him say, "and kill everybody else."

Dad is going to kill me, I thought. *I've become what he hates the most.*

We drove to the precinct, where I was escorted into a jail cell for minors. I was literally behind bars. I would never forget the sound of that metal door sealing me in.

It took about an hour for Dad to show up, but it felt like a year. I couldn't imagine life getting any worse. Once again I'd given him a reason to be upset with and disappointed in me.

Finally, I heard my dad's voice drift down the hall. He was explaining to the officers that he was a highway patrolman. He and two officers soon walked to my cell. The stare Dad gave me was unmistakable—he was embarrassed for himself and ashamed of me.

I am never going to be able to recover from this. I have completely failed.

Yet again I rode in the back seat of my dad's car as he drove me to Mom and Jeff's house. There was no conversation. When we arrived, Dad said, "Right now, I'm too angry to even talk to you." I got out without a word.

A couple of days later, Dad showed up at the end of one of our baseball practices at the high school. This time he was in uniform. We still hadn't talked about what happened. When practice finished, he called me over and we walked around the corner of a brick wall that lined a walkway between the baseball field and an apartment complex.

The moment we were out of sight of the other students, Dad put his hand on my chest and slammed me against the wall.

"I can't believe you embarrassed me like that," he said in a low tone. "I don't understand the way you're acting and the things you're getting involved in. You need to make some serious changes in your life."

I said nothing and showed no reaction, but my thoughts were racing. *I have no idea why I'm acting like this. I don't know why these things are happening.* All I understood was that I was incredibly angry.

Dad's hand pressed harder against my chest. "I'm ashamed of you and what you've done." Then he turned and walked away.

As I watched my father's retreating back, I was overwhelmed by the memory of that day in front of our house when he drove away, leaving me and my brothers in shock. It had been the most devastating moment of my young life, but another, even worse, would soon follow.

In the months after Dad's departure from our home, he kept promising to pick me up so I could spend the weekend with him at his new place. From my eight-year-old perspective, I decided that the only reason my father would leave me and the rest of his family was if he'd discovered something incredible. I believed he must live in a mansion or perhaps even better, something that compared to Disneyland. I'd been shaken to the core, but I held on to the hope that my dad had found an amazing new life. I couldn't wait to see him and learn what it was all about. I expected that everything would finally make sense.

The first two weekends that I was supposed to visit didn't work out, but at last, on a fall Friday, there he was after school in the familiar Chevy Malibu. He called through the open window, "Hey, how's it going?"

In the car, I practically bounced in my seat and asked rapid-fire questions: "What is your place like? Where is it? How is the furniture? I'm so excited to see it." Dad said little. We drove to an area not far from Jack Murphy Stadium, home of baseball's San Diego Padres, and approached a U-shaped two-story apartment complex that was partially hidden by a fence. When we pulled up to the gate, I saw that the apartments consisted of rows of beige stucco structures. I noticed cracks in some of the walls. I was surprised that the exterior was so unimpressive. I decided that the rooms must be phenomenal on the inside. We walked to number 8, Dad's ground-floor apartment. He walked in, with me following eagerly right behind, and flicked on a light.

I stared at the room in disbelief. The furniture consisted of an old vinyl couch, a used Formica table with two flimsy chairs, and a worn entertainment center with a few books on it. His TV stand was a piece of wood atop a pair of bricks. A lone window at the back of the apartment allowed a dim shaft of light in. In a dish drainer in the kitchen sink were a single glass, fork, knife, spoon, and plate. The white plate was trimmed with gold flowers; it was the only item I could see that didn't appear drab and shabby.

I had another reason for hoping that Dad's home would be something special. According to my grade school logic, I thought that *I* might be the cause of my parents' problems and divorce. I was the oldest child, after all. I knew there were times when I disappointed Dad. It made sense to me. Yet, if Dad had left us for a fantastic new situation, I might be able to let myself off the hook.

At the moment I saw Dad's apartment, however, I knew. He hadn't traded up at all. If this was what made him happy, I must have done something pretty terrible to drive him away. It was entirely my fault. I hadn't lived up to what my father expected of me. I had to accept the fact that I meant nothing to my dad. Because of what I'd done, I no longer had value in his eyes—or mine.

If anything, my fights and arrests since the divorce had only brought more shame and embarrassment to my dad. My life was spiraling out of control, but I couldn't talk about it. My hero had abandoned me and deemed me worthless. I kept my feelings to myself. I would never let anyone hurt me like that again.

I wished I could be happy. I wished I had something to hope for. I thought back to the summer before I started high school. The anger, tension, and feelings of worthlessness were such a contrast to what I'd experienced then. When I finished eighth grade, I still lived with Dad and Brenda, but Shane and Matt had left to stay with my mom and Gene, who had just moved to a rental home in Grants Pass, Oregon. The house was in a rural area on the Rogue River, which was known for its salmon runs, white-water rafting, and rugged scenery. My brothers told me about the opportunities for amazing adventures: fishing, hiking, building forts, catching snakes and night crawlers. I missed them and my mom, and I wasn't connecting with my dad. It was an easy decision to join them for the summer.

I had a blast exploring the Oregon outdoors with my brothers, but it wasn't my only great memory of that time. On one of my first days there, Mom dug in a side yard with a shovel while my brothers and I played in the backyard. A couple that looked in their seventies—the man wore overalls and a ball cap and the woman had on a flowered dress—walked up and introduced themselves to Mom. They were Al and Tina, our next-door neighbors.

"Are you thinking about putting in a garden?" Al asked.

"I am," Mom said. "The soil is so rich here. But I'm just going to start small with some tomatoes."

Al explained that he'd farmed some of his property and had gardens himself. "If you could do all that you wanted, how big would your garden be?" he asked.

Mom indicated an area that was probably twenty-five by seventy-five feet and mentioned planting cucumbers and beans along with the tomatoes. "Hopefully I can do that someday," she said. "But right now I'll just do what I can with this little patch here."

Al and Tina seemed like nice people. In fact, Tina brought us a bag of apricots and plums. But that didn't prepare me for what happened next.

The following morning, about six-thirty, a loose pane of glass in my bedroom window began rattling. It was accompanied by the sound of a motor. I rubbed sleep from my eyes and pulled back the curtain. To my surprise, there was Al, still wearing his overalls and ball cap, astride a John Deere tractor. He was skimming grass off the top of the ground in the area where Mom had wanted her garden. Once he pushed that grass into a pile, he lowered the rake in the back of his tractor and began tilling the soil.

I ran out of my bedroom and into the living room. Mom was watching Al through the front window. "I can't believe it," she said.

"He's tearing up the yard!" I said. I didn't understand what was happening.

Mom laughed. "No, he's tilling it for my garden," she said. "I'm going to have a garden!" Al saw us watching and tipped his hat.

"I can't believe he would do that for us," Mom said. "We don't have any money to give him." Based on our experience in California, people just didn't do things like that.

A couple of weeks later, Shane and I were practicing fly casting in the backyard, when we heard the doorbell ring. I dropped my fishing rod and ran into the house to answer the door. On our front step stood a man wearing a plaid shirt and round, wire-rim glasses. He was starting to go bald on top and had rosy cheeks and a big smile.

"Hi, what's your name?" he said.

My mom arrived, and after a minute of chatting, she invited the man in. Ernie Sackett was a friend of Al and Tina's. Mom served

Ernie berry cobbler that they ate in the living room as they talked. Shane, Matt, and I ate cobbler in the kitchen and eavesdropped.

Ernie got around to mentioning that he was the Sunday school teacher at the local church. "I live in that trailer park not far from here," he said. "I wonder if it would be all right with you if I picked up your boys on Sunday mornings and took them to Sunday school. We learn about Jesus Christ and all the Bible stories in my class."

Mom said she thought that was a great idea. I was actually kind of excited about the idea myself. Other than one Easter service with my grandmother years earlier, I'd never been to church. I'd heard a little about God but really had no concept of what or who he was. I thought I might like to find out.

I'd thought briefly about God back when Dad left us. I wasn't even sure if God was real, but if he was and Dad was mad at and disappointed in me, I figured God must be too. Now, though, I wondered if enough time had gone by. Maybe there was a chance he wasn't mad at me anymore.

The following Sunday morning, we heard the honk of a car horn. A brown four-door Buick was in our driveway. Ernie drove us to the church, which looked like something out of the *Little House on the Prairie* TV show—a white building with a steeple, mostly one big room with wooden pews. Our Sunday school class was in an attached room. That first morning, Ernie placed felt characters on a flannel board to tell the story of Joseph, the man who was left for dead by his brothers yet rose to become second-in-command in Egypt.

After class, we sat with Ernie in the pews for the church service. Al and Tina were there too. It was all a new experience for me. I didn't understand everything that Ernie and the pastor talked about, but I found it interesting. It helped that the people were so nice. I liked the after-church snacks too.

Ernie continued showing up at our house on Sunday mornings. On our fourth Sunday, after class, Ernie beckoned to me, Shane, and Matt. "Hey, you guys, come here," he said. "I have something for you." He handed each of us a cardboard box. When I opened mine, I saw a brown Bible with "Gregory Matthews" embossed in gold letters on the front. I opened it up and discovered colorful maps in the back and saw that Jesus's words were indicated in red throughout. This was a gift I would treasure for a long time.

Compared to my otherwise tumultuous adolescent years, that summer in Grants Pass was an oasis. The kindness and compassion demonstrated by Al, Tina, and Ernie to our family was unlike anything I'd seen before. They made me feel special. They acted as if I had value and a reason for existing. It was the opposite of what I usually felt when I was around Dad.

I also saw that Al, Tina, and Ernie believed in God. I had only just begun to think about whether or not he was real, but I sensed that *something* was out there. Ernie had talked about all of us being able to have a relationship with God. I wasn't sure what that meant, but if it led to the compassion and love that I'd experienced that summer, I was interested in finding out.

Unfortunately, after I moved back in with Dad and Brenda in San Diego, my memories of that magical summer faded while the anger and feelings of worthlessness came roaring back. I had to go to court after the DUI. My dad paid the fifteen-hundred-dollar fine, which I had to pay back with money earned from a part-time job. The court also prohibited me from getting a driver's license until I turned eighteen, a terrible blow to an almost-sixteen-year-old teenager.

Yet even those consequences weren't enough to derail my penchant for trouble. I got into more fights at school, including at the end of my sophomore year when I beat up four guys at once. When the principal pulled out my file after that one, it was an inch and a half thick.

That incident proved to be the last straw for the El Cajon administration. I was expelled from the school district. If I wanted to receive a high school diploma, I would have to enroll at Chaparral High, the alternative education continuation school in El Cajon. It was a place for students with academic and behavioral problems.

I couldn't seem to do anything right or please anyone, least of all my dad. I was mad at everyone, including myself. I felt ashamed. Even worse, I felt trapped. I was riding a fast train to oblivion and I saw no way to get off.

Little did I know that I was right where God wanted me.

6

SOMETHING'S OUT THERE

*Your enemy the devil prowls around like a roaring lion looking
for someone to devour.*
1 PETER 5:8 NIV

12:30 A.M. MONDAY, SEPTEMBER 21
KENAI PENINSULA, ALASKA

I had just settled into some well-deserved slumber. It felt as if every muscle and joint in my body was sore, so my descent into la-la land was a welcome relief. But it didn't last long. I realized that my cot was rocking in the evening darkness. Then a voice hissed: "Greg! Something's out there!"

I awoke in an instant, adrenaline coursing through my veins. I made out the outline of Matt sitting up in his cot. He was shaking my cot with his left hand. In his right hand was a pistol.

What was going on?

My day had begun at three-thirty that morning. I'd stepped out of the front door of Matt's house and shivered, partly because of the drizzle and thirty-four-degree temperature and partly because I was so eager to get our hunting adventure started. Matt and I made sure we had our wallets and hunting licenses. Then Matt remembered that Melinda had packed sandwiches and spaghetti for us in their freezer. We checked the straps holding down our gear in the truck and boat. Finally, we stood at the rear of Matt's truck and looked at each other.

"This is it," Matt said. "Do you think we have everything?"

"Yeah," I said. "I think we're as ready as we're ever going to be."

Matt slapped the bed of the truck. "All right. Here we go."

The drive to our destination on the Kenai Peninsula was six hours of increasingly dazzling scenery. We took Alaska Route 1 and soon arrived in Anchorage, the state's largest city at three hundred thousand people. Anchorage's few tall buildings—the highest was twenty-two stories—were dwarfed by the Chugach Mountains to the east. We had one stop to make—I still hadn't purchased any bear spray. I wanted a can that came with a holster so I'd have quick access if needed. I found what I was looking for at a sporting goods store.

From the city, we traveled south, then southeast along the edge of Turnagain Arm, a narrow waterway to the east of Cook Inlet. On our left, rugged mountains stretched precipitously toward the sky. Their highest point, at more than five thousand feet, was South Suicide Peak. The contrast of black rock and white snow on its flanks gave the mountain a majestic and forbidding appearance.

I turned my head to the right. The highway was so close to the aquamarine waterline that I almost felt as if I were on a boat. Along one stretch, Matt pointed out the spray of gray whales on the water's surface. Later, a low tide revealed vast mudflats. A handful of people armed with buckets and clam tubes scoured the beach for the tasty mollusks. It looked no more dangerous than the clam digging we used to do in San Diego, but newcomers to the area sometimes wandered far out into the flats and were caught in the soupy mud and sand, which acted like quicksand. Unable to free themselves, they were trapped in a watery grave when the tide rushed back in. In Alaska, even a seemingly routine activity like clamming could turn deadly.

We eventually reached the end of the arm and turned southwest. Now we were on the Kenai Peninsula itself. Roughly two hundred miles long and one hundred miles wide, the peninsula was home to ice fields, the glacier-covered Kenai Mountains, and numerous lakes and rivers filled with salmon. For millennia, Dena'ina Indians made the peninsula their home, as did Alutiiqs in the south and Chugaches in the east. They subsisted on the bounty of fish and wildlife available in this fertile region. I hoped it was my turn to participate in this centuries-old tradition.

As we drove deeper into the heart of the peninsula, I observed some of the most breathtaking landscapes on the planet. Miles of dense green forest reminded me of an endless ocean. Towering, jagged mountain ranges made me feel insignificant. Alaska revealed a little more of herself with every mile. She was strikingly beautiful, but I knew that beneath the lovely exterior was a fickle and sometimes unforgiving spirit. Alaska held life in one hand and death in the other, and you didn't always know which she would reveal next.

We'd been driving about three hours when we reached Cooper Landing, a village of about three hundred people staked out at the western end of Kenai Lake. Log cabins and lodges competed with evergreen trees for space. The heavily forested region attracted hunters, fishermen, and adventurers. This was the last outpost of civilization we would encounter. From here, we would travel along remote roads even farther into the interior, until we reached our destination: the widening of the mighty Kenai River known as Skilak Lake.

While Matt drove, I shot video of the sights and added commentary so that later our families could also enjoy our exploits. I glanced

over and saw Matt grin. He was enjoying showing off his home state
to his big brother. My "little" brother was actually a gentle giant, six-
foot-four and strong as a tank. He was a man of few words but an
excellent woodsman. I was grateful that I could count on him if we
found ourselves in a tight spot.

We arrived at Skilak's upper-side boat ramp in the late afternoon,
traveling the last four miles by dirt road. I jumped out of the truck and
did a 360-degree turn to take in the surroundings. The sun was out
now, adding depth to the mountains and highlighting the greens and
golds of the pine and aspen trees that lined the lakeshore. Directly in
front of us were a rocky beach and a wide, primitive boat ramp that
descended into the water. Skilak Lake was the termination point of the
Kenai River, though it was also fed by runoff from Skilak Glacier. The
lake was fifteen miles long and up to four miles wide. In a couple more
months it would be frozen over, but today the water was clear. For the
next ten days, we would call this beautiful sliver of Alaska our home.

Matt and I checked and rearranged the placement of our gear in
the boat—if the nose was too heavy, it might torpedo the boat into
the water and sink us. Finally, Matt looked satisfied. "We are ready,
brother," he said. "Let's do this."

The wind had increased, whipping up whitecaps on the water
that were visible for miles. But I trusted Matt when he said the surface conditions wouldn't be an issue. He was proud of his new boat.
It was a twenty-six-foot Alumaweld jet sled with a center console,
windshield, and two seats, a boat that had proven itself many times
amid the rigors of the Alaskan wilderness. He'd installed a loran and
GPS, which would tell us the depth of the water we'd be exploring
and our exact location.

I was almost giddy as I stood in the water in hip boots and helped
Matt ease the boat down the ramp and into the lake. In minutes, we

were off. An hour later, as the sun set, the bow of our boat slid gently
to a halt on a rocky shoreline at the southwest section of the lake,
near Caribou Island.

We had arrived.

The beach consisted of about eight feet of smooth, fist-sized rocks
which ended at a line of thick, mossy brush and a wall of pine trees. I
was holding the rope while Matt shut the engine down when I heard
a scream from above. An eagle soared over us and then dove into the
water, talons outstretched, as it sought a trout for dinner. This was
a nature lover's paradise, but I knew that hidden somewhere within
the forest before us were creatures more dangerous than an eagle.
I grabbed the loaded shotgun and Matt unholstered his pistol. We
walked into the timber to search for a place to set up camp.

About fifty feet from shore, we found a relatively flat area. "Well,
this is an option," Matt said. We hiked another quarter mile, continu-
ally scanning the area for potential predators as well as for more flat
or open space. Nothing better materialized. Our first option would
have to do.

Now the real work started. We began unloading our supplies and
hauling them up to our selected area. It took close to two hours. I
was exhausted and we hadn't even begun to establish our base camp.

Our first order of business was choosing a site for the shotgun.
From now on, anytime we were in camp during the day, we'd both
know where to run if something caught us by surprise and we had to
defend ourselves.

While Matt used a chain saw to clear the camp area, I put together
our cabin and equipment storage tents. The twelve-by-twelve-foot
cabin tent included a rain fly that was rated to carry a snow load,
just in case. In addition, this expeditionary tent had a four-foot ves-
tibule at the front for hanging and drying wet gear. We also had a

twenty-by-twenty-foot tarp to cover the kitchen area. I'd done a ton of research on how to set up our kitchen. We had a four-burner stove and griddle plumbed with seven gallons of propane. We had a three-gallon collapsible water jug with attached faucet for drinking water. We would fill a washtub with boiling water to wash dishes. I cut the lower branches on a pine sapling down to one-inch stubs to use as our kitchen cabinet. The water jug, pots, pans, and cooking utensils were hung at eye level. Dry goods, paper products, a coffeemaker, spices, and other cooking implements were stored in plastic bins that slid under a six-foot folding table. Kerosene hurricane lamps lit the kitchen and our walking paths throughout the camp.

We set up our food storage area about seventy-five feet away—far enough so animals wouldn't be parading through our camp but close enough so we could defend our food if necessary.

At this point we were losing light fast, so we located our head-lamps and a spare set of batteries. I had just filled my pockets with batteries when I heard a series of howls—wolves. With the evening darkness nearly upon us, a confrontation with a wolf pack was the last thing I wanted. Fortunately, the sound was distant. I hoped it stayed that way.

Once the kitchen, sleeping area, and equipment storage were set up, it was time to finish clearing the camp of fallen dead trees, which would become our fuel supply for fires. The sound of the chain saw echoed across the surface of the lake and bounced off the mountains behind us. I'm sure the growling motor could be heard for miles. It seemed wrong to disturb the beauty of Alaska with such a foreign noise. Staying warm and having the ability to dry clothes and boots were a priority, however. At 10 p.m., Matt shut down the chain saw and laid it next to the towering pile of firewood. We were exhausted and hungry.

Dinner and a cozy bedroll were calling, but one last task remained. Matt and I had discussed many times how we would secure our camp. I'd purchased a thousand feet of four-hundred-pound fishing line that was normally used to string decoys together for duck hunting. Matt had brought a couple dozen aluminum cans. We filled each of the cans with more than forty steel BBs, then strung the fishing line through them. Moving out about fifty feet from the center of the campsite, I chose a tree and secured one end of the fishing line approximately two feet up the base of the trunk. While walking backwards with the spool of line in my hand, I began circling the camp, stopping every few feet to wrap the line around trees. Matt slid the cans down the fishing line and positioned two or three of them between each tree. Once we had the cans set, we pulled the heavy fishing line until it was taut and secured it. Anything that came through at night would strike the fishing line and send the cans into a cacophony of jangling steel.

Close to midnight, we finished our cold sandwiches under the dim light of a hurricane lantern and slid into our tent. Our Outfitters tent was far better equipped than what we'd had with Dad on our summer trips. This tent accommodated individual extra-wide cots, double Therm-a-Rest sleeping pads, comfortable pillows, and zero-degree sleeping bags. We even installed a tent reading light that came in handy when getting dressed to go out at night to use the pit toilet, which was down a little trail forty feet from the campsite.

I was proud of our planning and how it had all come together. When we finally bedded down, I was beat, yet my mind raced with anticipation of what the next day would bring. I fell asleep talking to Matt about our camp and the hunting we would do in the following days.

When Matt shook me awake, however, I suddenly wondered if our preparations had been enough. Something had tripped our BB-can predator alarm.

The metal rattling had stopped. The shotgun was between us, leaning against the back wall of the tent. Trying to stay as quiet as possible, I reached over and brought the shotgun to my chest, careful to point the business end in a safe direction. Both of us kept silent and listened for the slightest sound. Despite my heavy breathing, I could have heard a pin drop outside.

Thirty minutes passed before we finally relaxed. Whatever had tried to enter our perimeter had apparently been scared off by our rattling steel contraption. I put the shotgun down and drifted off yet again, though less easily this time. What had triggered our makeshift alarm just fifty feet away? A squirrel? A wolf? Something even bigger? I couldn't help wondering.

That night, neither Matt nor I knew that three people on the peninsula had been attacked by bears in separate incidents over the past three months. The last attack occurred just a week earlier when a grizzly mauled a man walking a dog near the Kenai River. He was flown by medevac to a hospital and placed in intensive care with major injuries.

If I had known about the bear attacks, I might not have gone back to sleep at all.

7

PUZZLE PIECES

Sometimes the hardest pieces of a puzzle to assemble are the ones missing from the box.
—DIXIE WATERS

I sat on a wooden pew in my Ocean Pacific polo shirt and Levi's 501 jeans and squirmed. Shane sat next to me, wearing similar attire and looking as uncomfortable as I felt. We were in the last row of a San Diego church. In the pews ahead of us, more than fifty high school kids huddled together, chatting and laughing.

I can't wait to get through this, I thought. *I can't wait to be done with church and get back home so we can do something fun.*

I was not here by choice. During my sophomore year of high school, I'd been living with Mom and Jeff. Then I'd moved in with the family of my girlfriend at the time. After the fight that got me expelled from the district, however, both that living arrangement and that relationship ended. Dad was furious at me about the fight, which made moving in with him and Brenda less than appealing. That left Mom and Jeff. My brothers were there, so it made some sense. And my new stepdad was a pretty relaxed guy, easier to be around than my dad.

The problem, from my perspective, was that Jeff was a Christian. Though Mom hadn't made any faith commitment yet, she was intrigued by Christianity. Both Jeff and Mom were going to church regularly. They made me an offer: I could move in with them again, but only if I agreed to go to church every Sunday.

I didn't want to do it. My introduction to God with Ernie, Al, and Tina in Grants Pass two summers before seemed like a distant memory. Everything in my life had gone downhill since then. I was once again sure that God had to be as mad at and disappointed in me as my dad was. Going to church sounded like a waste of time. But I didn't have a lot of options. Reluctantly, I agreed to Mom and Jeff's plan.

That Sunday morning when Shane and I sat in a back-row pew was my second with the high school group. I didn't know any of these people. Based on the upscale neighborhood and the Mercedes and BMWs in the parking lot, this was a different and more affluent crowd than what I was used to, definitely from the other side of the tracks. I didn't think I fit in.

The youth leader, Barry, stood at the front of the sanctuary and started talking about an upcoming event. Out of boredom, I examined the hymnal, paper, and pen in the rack attached to the back of the pew in front of me. I noticed movement to my right, glanced quickly in that direction, then dropped my head again.

Wait, what was that?

I looked up once more. Three of the most attractive girls I'd ever seen had just walked into Sunday school and were taking seats only two rows in front of us. The girls all wore fall dresses. They were all slender and tan. They moved with the natural grace of athletes. One in particular caught my attention, however. She appeared to be the oldest. This girl wore a white dress with a flower print and spaghetti straps and had curly chestnut hair that fell to the middle of her back.

All right, I thought. *Things are looking up. Now if I get bored I'll at least have something to look at.*

Shane and I sat through the rest of the gathering, which included a message from the church youth leader and singing of worship songs that we didn't know the words to. Finally, the meeting was over. Just before we were dismissed, the leader announced that in the afternoon there would be pizza and a softball game at a local park for anyone interested.

As Shane and I walked out, we passed the three girls, who were now standing and talking with one another. The girl in the white dress turned toward me. She had gorgeous brown eyes.

"Hey, are you guys going to play softball?" she asked.

I stopped mid-stride. *My gosh, she's talking to me.* I didn't know what to say. I didn't know what my mom's schedule was for the day and if we'd be able to get a ride to the park. But the words that came out of my mouth were "Yes, we're going."

"Good," the girl said with a smile. "Looking forward to seeing you out there."

Suddenly I was very interested in playing softball with the church youth group. Fortunately, Mom was available to drive us. I had her drop off Shane and me a couple blocks from the park—Mom's car was a piece of junk, which was definitely not the impression I was going for. Soon we were all gathered around pizzas spread out on a picnic table. I found myself standing next to the girl with the gorgeous eyes, who now wore shorts, a white tank top, and a visor over hair pulled back in a ponytail. I learned that her name was Janelle. The youth leader said he would offer a blessing and asked everyone to hold hands, so I took Janelle's hand. When the blessing was done, I held on a little longer than necessary. Janelle didn't seem to mind.

During the game, Janelle played shortstop and I played third base. In between batters we had a chance to talk and get to know each other a bit. By the time the afternoon was over, I was sure that the attraction I felt was mutual. When Janelle asked if I would be going to the Wednesday night youth group, I had no idea what that was about, but there was no question in my mind that I would be there.

Janelle attended a private high school and I was going to the Chaparral continuation school, so we didn't see each other on weekdays. But it wasn't long before I was sitting with Janelle and holding her hand every Sunday morning and Wednesday night. I was hooked.

I was also intrigued by what I was hearing at church. At the end of each Wednesday night meeting, Barry talked about the truth found in the Bible's gospel message and about Jesus—that he loved each of us so much that he gave his life for us. It sounded like a love that would never leave you and never hurt you. It was the kind of love I thought I had as a kid until that moment I watched my dad drive away.

I still wasn't convinced, however, that Jesus could love me like that. I'd made too many mistakes and let my dad down. Surely I had let God down too. I didn't see how he could overlook everything I'd done.

The last thing Barry did on those Wednesday nights was invite anyone who wanted to give their heart to Jesus to come forward. Part of me wanted to stand, walk to the front of the room, and do exactly that. Yet I was conflicted, so I held back. I'd given my heart away before and been burned. I needed to know more.

* * *

A COUPLE OF MONTHS AFTER we met, I sat with Janelle during a Sunday service. She suddenly leaned over and whispered, "Hey, my parents would like you to come over for lunch."

I was instantly terrified. I'd met Janelle's parents before, but this was taking things to a new level. I'd shared a little about my background with Janelle. She knew my parents were divorced and that I'd lived on my own. But I was afraid to reveal too much, especially to her parents. They were committed Christians and I wasn't. They might say, "No, you two can't see each other anymore."

Yet I couldn't think of a good excuse to decline the lunch offer. An hour later, we pulled into a long driveway that led to a well-kept split-level home. Janelle parked and put her hand on my knee. "Hey, don't be nervous," she said. "You'll love my parents."

It turned out she was right. When Janelle's mom, Sandy, greeted us at the door, she threw her arms around me and said, "I'm so glad you're here. Welcome to our home." Her husband, Dave, seemed just as pleased to spend time with me.

I was struck by this family's obvious faith in God. It seemed as if there was a Bible in every room. Scripture verses were posted on the fridge. They prayed before every meal. It was so different from anything I'd been around before. I could sense a spiritual presence in that home.

It wasn't long before I was spending a lot of time at Janelle's house. Sandy and I sometimes talked about my God questions. She'd pull out a Bible and turn to a specific verse to guide her answer. What she said made sense. One inch at a time, my heart was opening the door to the idea that Jesus and his love were real.

I was at Janelle's house one day when Sandy said, "There's a pastor who's going to be speaking in town in a couple of days. He has the gift of prophecy. Would you like to go with me and hear him?"

I wasn't sure what to think of a guy who claimed to hear from God. I was still digesting what I was learning about prophets who lived centuries ago, during Old Testament times. But I trusted Sandy. Everything I'd seen and heard so far with her family felt right.

"Sure," I said. "I'll go."

Janelle was at work that day, so just Sandy and I attended the pastor's talk at a local church. After delivering his message, the pastor invited people to come forward to be "prayed over." Sandy wanted to do it, so we joined about thirty people in line. When we reached the front of the line, we stepped onto the stage. The pastor, a clean-shaven, sixtyish man in a white shirt and gray sport coat, put his hand on Sandy's head and said a prayer. I stood behind Sandy and tried to blend in. I was only there to support Sandy. I wasn't planning on talking to the pastor myself.

When the pastor finished praying, however, he turned toward me. "Who is this?" he asked. Sandy introduced me.

"Come closer," the pastor said. "I have a word for you."

I wasn't sure what a "word" meant, but I stepped forward. The pastor put a hand on my shoulder.

"You are a man like David," he said. "You're a man after God's own heart."

I don't know what I expected to happen—maybe that the pastor would offer a piece of spiritual advice that I could go home and ponder. Instead, however, it was like he'd set off a bomb inside me. I had held back so much pain for such a long time. For some reason it was suddenly pouring out. I began to sob and couldn't stop. I was overwhelmed. Sandy put her arm around me and we walked off the stage.

But there was even more to it than that. I didn't comprehend it at the time, but a man who didn't know me had put into words what would become my foremost desire. That simple sentence—"You're a man after God's own heart"—was both exhortation and forecast. For the first time, I could picture myself as a person who belonged to and with God. I somehow knew that I would spend the rest of my days seeking his will for my life.

I considered the pastor's words often over the next several days. I also looked up David in the Bible and read about some of the powerful ways that God had worked in his life. I knew that there was something tangible here.

At Wednesday night youth group about two weeks after Sandy and I visited the pastor, Barry as usual ended the meeting with an altar call. The music died down and the lights dimmed as he said, "I sense that there are some people here who need to get right with the Lord or accept the Lord. Don't be afraid of what God is telling you. If you want to receive the Lord, just come forward."

The same feeling I'd had when the pastor spoke to me began welling up inside. I saw one person stand and go to the front of the church, and then another. I felt a sense of destiny, that this night was meant to be. Then I heard an inaudible, insistent voice: *You need to go. You need to go. You need to go.*

I stood and walked to the front of the room. Soon Barry and another staff member were talking to me. "Do you understand what this is about?" Barry asked. "Do you want to accept Jesus Christ as your savior?"

I did. Once again, I was overwhelmed by emotion. I shed a few tears, but the sensation was different from what I'd experienced two weeks earlier. So many thoughts and feelings ran through me. My heart was full. I felt peace. Maybe my past did not have to dictate my future. Maybe there really was a higher sense of authority than my dad. Instead of feeling ashamed, maybe I could feel pardoned and all my mistakes could be washed away.

I still had a thousand questions. I knew my relationship with Jesus was only just beginning and that I had a lot to learn. But I was thrilled. I had taken the first step of the journey.

DURING MY FINAL YEAR OF studies at Chaparral, I thought more and more about what I should do with my life. Considering my lack of academic success, my career options seemed limited. I respected my dad's service as a police officer, but I didn't want to follow in his footsteps. I'd always known that he had a dangerous job and I had always been afraid that he would come home hurt—or, worse, not come home at all. I didn't want the people close to me to worry like that, to wonder if I would make it home from work. Yet it was important to me to do something to help and protect people. As the oldest child, I'd always been protective of my brothers. That inclination was still part of me.

In the fall of that last year, at the suggestion of my stepmom, I visited a local fire station. I'd never even thought about firefighting, but just seeing the big red fire engine parked in front of the bay doors was impressive. I cornered a lieutenant and started asking questions. He invited me to come back if I was interested in learning more, which I did. Within a week I knew that this was the kind of work I wanted to do.

I began reading up and training to become a reserve firefighter. Just a few weeks after that initial visit, I qualified to start day shifts at the station. At this point, Dad and I were at least speaking to each other. We just didn't talk about what had happened in the past. I'd buried the bad feelings and hurt as best I could. I still desperately wanted him to approve of me, which was another reason why firefighting appealed to me. I knew Dad would be pleased.

A couple days before my first shift, I called Dad and said, "Hey, you guys have got to come down and see what I've been working on." Dad and Brenda met me at the station on the morning of that first shift. I was giving them a tour of the facility, when the alarm tones went off. My first call! Dad later told me that my eyes were as big as saucers when I climbed onto the rig. He waved as we left the station. In that instant, I believed he was proud of me. It was a great moment.

I continued my training and was certified as both a California state firefighter and a national registered emergency medical technician (EMT). After two years of working as a reserve, I hoped to land a full-time firefighting position with the city of San Diego. I aced the physical agility test and out of roughly two thousand candidates was ranked near the top of their list. But in my interview, I was told that I just didn't have enough experience to qualify. It was a major disappointment.

A friend suggested I consider firefighting in the military. I did some research and liked what the air force offered. The more I looked at it, the more it seemed to make sense. At the end of my four-year enlistment, I'd be qualified to serve with any fire department in the country.

I also knew that it would make Dad happy. When I signed the papers, I was twenty years old.

On the cool December morning that I had to report to the Military Entrance Processing Station in San Diego, Dad picked me up at four-thirty. During that short drive in the dark, we had one of the most meaningful conversations between us in my life. He told me about how nervous he was when he joined the Marine Corps. He said he thought I was doing the right thing and that he was impressed by the decisions I was making for my life. When we stopped at the station, Dad turned to me, smiled, and said, "You know what? I'm just really proud of you."

I basked in those long-sought words of approval. I felt like that little boy hanging out with his dad again, before everything fell apart. When we got out of the car, I gave Dad a big hug. He said, "I know you're going to be awesome at this." It gave me confidence to take on the big, scary world I was about to face.

I would replay that conversation many times in the years that followed. Whenever I faced an important decision, even though Dad wasn't there physically, I asked myself, *What do you think about this, Dad? Are you proud of me? Is this what you want me to do?* I wanted Dad to say it was okay.

In truth, though, I was after something else even more. I didn't have the courage to ask, but I longed for Dad to take me in his arms and forgive me for driving him away.

BEING WITH JANELLE WAS WONDERFUL, and both she and her family had done so much to point me in the right direction spiritually. But it became clear after we both earned our high school diplomas that our lives were on different paths. Janelle intended to go to college to be a doctor. I was starting to get excited about a career in firefighting. We parted ways, trusting that we would get back together if it was meant to be and thankful for what we had shared.

In fall 1987, when I was twenty, another firefighter introduced me to a friend of his girlfriend. Mary Jo was a soft-spoken tomboy who loved horses, working on cars, and camping. She was also a Christian. I loved that she enjoyed the outdoors and could take care of herself. We hit it off right away.

Our relationship progressed quickly. Once I decided to join the air force, it felt as if everything in my life was playing at fast-forward. Mary Jo seemed a natural fit, another piece of the puzzle. I realized I wanted a companion to join me on the exciting and daunting journey I was about to begin.

In February 1988, I returned to San Diego after basic training. One day Mary Jo and I drove to the Ocean Beach area. As the sun set and the waves broke against the sand, we took a walk on the pier. To Mary Jo's surprise, I suddenly got down on one knee and pulled a small box out of my pocket. "I don't know what being in the military is going to be like," I said, "but I know I'm going to have a career that could take care of us. I really would like to have you by my side. Would you accompany me on this adventure and be my wife?"

With her eyes shining, Mary Jo threw her arms around me. "Yes," she said. "Absolutely!"

In May, I completed my training at the U.S. Air Force Fire Academy near Chicago. Later that month, we married in a San Diego church, and after a brief honeymoon I reported to my first air force duty assignment in Fairford, England. Mary Jo joined me a couple of months later.

After all I'd been through, I almost wanted to pinch myself. It appeared I had somehow managed to break away from the awful, seemingly inevitable course that my life had been on. The picture I imagined for my future finally looked more like an idyllic postcard instead of a grainy mug shot. I felt as if my struggles were over.

What I didn't understand was that almost everything I was doing was based on a lie and a buried but deeply felt place of pain. My struggles were actually only just beginning.

8

ALL IN

We entered the land you sent us to explore, and it is indeed a
bountiful country—a land flowing with milk and honey.
—NUMBERS 13:27 NLT

5:15 A.M., MONDAY, SEPTEMBER 21
SKILAK LAKE

Streaks of pink and red stretched low across the horizon. Skilak Lake was perfectly still, its surface a mirror reflecting images of pine trees rising up to the mountains. It was the morning after Matt and I had been startled by the unknown intruder activating our predator alarm. Any misgivings I'd had the previous night were already forgotten. I was just thankful that God had allowed me to be here for this moment. I couldn't wait to get into the wilderness. It was time to hunt.

Ice crunched under the weight of our feet with each step aboard the jet boat. The final pieces of equipment were loaded and secured. With a turn of the key, the boat's engine sprang to life. We slowly motored east, keeping close to the lake's south shore. There was no place to tie up here. Steep granite rock faces rose more than twenty feet out of the water, the view broken in spots by pine trees that had taken root within cracks in the formations. Farther up from shore, the granite landscape gave way to draws, meadows, and forested hills, which even higher up yielded to mountains. For the wildlife that lived in this region, the days were growing shorter and the nights colder. All of the signs that summer was coming to an end were present. The mountains were decorated in an array of colors, starting from deep green at their baseline and extending up to a dizzying mix of orange, blue, purple, and red.

When Matt sighted a promising location, he turned off the engine and I grabbed my Swarovski binoculars. We each took our positions in the swiveling captain's chairs and glassed the vast landscape. We traced the meadows, the forest, and the ridgelines for any movement that might reveal a moose in hiding—the flick of an ear or the glint of an antler. After an hour with no luck, Matt started the boat and we moved farther east.

Each stop on the water turned out like the last. At one point I was treated to the sight of an eagle diving into the lake for a salmon, but onshore not a creature was stirring. Matt and I took our lunch break, downing sandwiches and Gatorade. We even pulled out our fishing poles and trolled for trout and salmon. But our fishing efforts weren't any more successful than our big-game scouting.

I hadn't expected to see the perfect bull moose in our first twenty minutes away from camp. But I figured after hours of scanning that we'd see *something*, even if it was only a deer. "What is going on here?" I said. "Where are the game?"

I had to remind myself that the country before me was virtually endless. We were concentrating on areas only two or three hundred yards from the water. But the sloping terrain stretched seemingly to the sky. The animals we sought might easily be five miles away.

I reluctantly realized that I would have to be patient.

Sometime after lunch, we aimed the bow of the jet boat toward Doroshin Bay at the northeast corner of the lake. Here were opportunities to bring the boat ashore. By the time our craft slid onto a polished-stone beach, it was 3 p.m. Where had the day gone? The sun was already making its downward course toward the western horizon. The massive mountains of the Alaska Range, which included Denali, North America's highest summit at more than twenty thousand feet, appeared to reach up to drag the yellow orb behind the range's jagged peaks. They would not wait for us.

From our seats in the jet boat, leaning back against our life vests, my brother and I again scanned the area beyond the shoreline. The more I observed, the more excited I became. Just a hundred yards away was the edge of a five-acre pond that had formed because of a heavily fortified beaver dam. Young grasses and roots filled the edges of the pond. I was sure that many a moose had submerged its huge head and rack in the icy water in order to pull up the tender roots. Beyond the pond, a valley extended up into the hills. A small creek wound its way along the valley floor toward the pond. Young willows, a favored food source for moose, traced the course of the creek. The whole area was made up of the boggy terrain and thick vegetation that moose loved.

The setting looked like every wilderness YouTube video and the pictures in every hunting magazine article I had ever seen. This was moose country. I was sure this was the place where I would have my chance to outsmart this North American giant.

I scanned the area on the left while Matt glassed the section on the right. For many long minutes, as before, all was still. Then Matt stiffened. "I've got something, Greg. About three-quarters up the ridgeline in that stand of blueberries. I think it's a bear."

I shifted my binoculars to the direction Matt was pointing. About three thousand feet above the lake, at the transition point between orange and yellow vegetation below and granite covered by a layer of purple moss-like growth, was a long band of blueberry bushes. With the help of Matt's instruction, I found the exact spot he indicated. There *was* something dark there.

Then the something raised its head. I took in the familiar rounded ears, the orange snout, and a frame that probably supported three hundred pounds of meat and muscle. No doubt, this was a black bear.

The prize I most wanted was a bull moose, of course. But Matt and I had purchased black bear tags as well. I knew there was no guarantee we'd even see a moose in Alaska, let alone bag one. I also knew how much Matt and his family appreciated bear meat. If I could help provide for them for the winter, I was ready and willing. We still had eight days to find a moose.

I had been waiting two years to scratch my big-game-hunting itch and now I had a bear in my sights. "We should get it," I said. "Let's stalk it."

Matt rubbed his chin and looked at the valley. "Well," he said, "we might be able to get up there before dark. But after we shot it, skinned it, and quartered it, we'd be carrying it out in darkness. That is definitely asking for trouble from predators."

I immediately realized that my brother, the experienced Alaska hunter, was right. We were hunting in an environment where *we* were part of the food chain. Reluctantly, I agreed that we should return before first light and relocate the bear. We could traverse the ridgeline and be in position for the shot just as the sun was breaking over the mountains.

Matt and I spent more time scanning the area in preparation for the morning. Although I was excited about the possibility of stalking the bear, my mind soon returned to the idea of hunting moose. I knew from what I'd seen through the binoculars that the terrain was rugged and would not be easily traversed. Sadly, moose preferred anything that was the opposite of easy. The thicker, wetter, muddier, and soggier the ground was, the more the moose liked it. If you really wanted to bag a moose, all you had to do was fight your way into the most inaccessible area possible, then wait. Of course, this decision had to be tempered by the fact that on your way through this inhospitable terrain, you would be carrying thirty to forty pounds of gear, water, and food. You'd be dirty, wet, exhausted, and covered with mosquitoes with the day barely begun. If your skills as a big-game hunter did pay off, your reward would be spending the next eight hours cleaning and hauling close to a thousand pounds of meat on your back through the previously mentioned muck. Not to mention that you wouldn't be the only predator in the neighborhood that enjoyed moose meat. Both wolves and bears hunted moose as part of their regular diet. What better way to enjoy a meal than to let someone else kill it for you?

As I continued to examine every detail of the valley, I counted the personal costs of making my way to that perfect hunting spot, conducting my hunt, and then, if fate would have it, shouldering my prize for trip after the exhausting trip back to the boat. I'd already invested over seven thousand dollars, and the physical effort that would be required was enormous. Yet for me there was no doubt that even having a chance at success made it worth it. Part of it was the opportunity to fulfill my dream of a triumphant big-game hunt in Alaska. Another part was the chance to test myself against one of nature's iconic mammals with a weapon from centuries past, the bow and arrow. Still another motivation was the pure joy of sharing the adventure with my brother. In a way, it would complete the plans for outdoor adventure that Shane, Matt, and I had made in my room that summer so many years ago.

I put down my binoculars and glanced at the front of the boat where my compound bow rested in a zippered case. I was going after a bull moose with a bow. Was this really a good idea? The animal I intended to confront might stand seven or eight feet at the shoulders and be armed with a rack of pointed antlers six or seven feet across. I had been practicing intensely to place an arrow in a fist-sized target from thirty-five to forty yards away. I hoped to be within twenty-five yards before I shot. I didn't want the moose to suffer. I wanted a clean kill.

But what if my shot was off the mark? A wounded moose was likely to charge in whatever direction he was facing, taking out anything that lay in his path, whether it was trees or men.

Again, however, I knew that my answer had not changed. I wanted the additional challenge and risk of hunting with a bow. This was what being a man was about. I felt like a gunfighter in a smoky saloon at a dimly lit poker table. I was pushing forward a mountain of chips, unholstering my Colt revolver and laying it on the table, and then reaching into my vest pocket to flip my last twenty-dollar gold piece onto the pile. I was all in.

About 5:30 p.m., the wind picked up and the temperature dropped in a hurry. We could have stayed longer to scout with our binoculars for game, but we knew we were already facing a headwind and whitecaps on the ride back to our base camp. Discussion soon turned to the pound-and-a-half rib-eye steaks waiting for us in our cooler and how good they would be with some fried red garlic potatoes and onions. It was time to go.

Just before dark, we beached the boat near our camp and tied the mooring lines to a pair of trees onshore. Matt and I grabbed our headlamps and fired up the kerosene lamps. The camp came to life. All the hard work we'd put into planning our setup was now paying off. Matt threw a couple of logs in the fire ring. For the Matthews brothers, there would be no rubbing two sticks together to get a fire started. Matt picked up a propane roofing torch—the blue flame ignited with a pop. Within three minutes, the burning logs were putting out some serious heat. I reached into one of the kitchen bins under the table, pulled out a stainless steel barbecue grill, and laid it over the fire. While the grill heated up, I broke out the cast-iron frying pan, spices, red potatoes, and onions. I lit the two kerosene lanterns that were strung above the cooking table and before long the smells of ambrosia wafted across our noses. After basting the steaks with a light covering of olive oil, I rubbed them with a special blackened Cajun spice mix I'd concocted just for this trip. This would be a meal to remember.

The evening was perfect. Matt and I sat next to the crackling fire and watched the steaks sizzle on the grill. The smell of the Cajun spices rose and mixed with the smoke of our fire into the stillness of the Alaska night. Once dinner preparations were complete, our camp was plunged into a silence interrupted only by the sound of smacking lips and guttural, carnivorous groans. Maybe it was being in the outdoors, but steak had never tasted so good.

I went to bed that night feeling both satisfied and full of anticipation. Tomorrow our hunting would begin in earnest. Matt and I had so much to learn from each other. We both looked forward to the opportunity to reconnect and bond as brothers. Neither of us realized we would soon be forced to bond with each other in a way we'd never expected.

REJECTION

You are God my stronghold. Why have you rejected me?
—PSALM 43:2 NIV

"**I** need to talk to you."

It was nine in the morning on a cloudy June day in 1994. My shift at the fire station had ended, I'd just returned to our small home in North Bend, Washington, and I was reaching for the coffeepot. Mary Jo leaned against the wall a few feet away from me. My wife wore jeans, a T-shirt, and tennis shoes, her casual housework attire. The hands on her hips and the look in her eyes, however, told me this wasn't going to be a casual conversation.

"Sure, let's talk," I said. "What's up?"

"I need a straight answer from you."

I stared at her for a moment. "Are you okay?"

Mary Jo looked down. "No," she said. She shook her head. "No, I'm not okay. I'm really not okay."

I took a deep breath. I had a feeling I knew where this was going.

Mary Jo raised her head again and locked eyes with mine. "Think carefully about the answer you give to the question I'm about to ask you." Her voice cracked as she struggled to get out the words: "Are we going to have kids together?"

I swallowed. I knew how badly Mary Jo wanted children. How many times had we discussed it during our seven years together, especially lately? Her biological alarm clock was definitely ringing. Having a family and realizing the joy of motherhood meant everything to her.

I wanted to say yes to her question, I really did. Mary Jo would be a great mom. But me, a dad? I was convinced that no matter how good their intentions and no matter how hard they tried, fathers brought pain to their children. Dad had done it with me. I knew I would do it too.

Since completing my air force enlistment and joining Eastside Fire and Rescue, I'd seen it with my own eyes. It was only two weeks ago that I'd waited down the street with a medic unit while police officers and county sheriff's deputies responded to an incident at a residence. The family, we were told, had a history of domestic violence.

After fifteen minutes, a deputy had stepped into the middle of the street and frantically waved us in. His eyes were red. We donned our gloves and protective glasses, grabbed our trauma kits, and rushed inside. A metal lunchbox, unopened, sat on the kitchen table. A second officer stood nearby, rubbing his eyes with his head down.

We were all too late.

The scene was brutal—blood everywhere, three bodies in the living room, and a fourth in a back bedroom. A quick check confirmed that the three in the living room—a mother and two daughters—

were dead. They'd been stabbed to death. The fourth body was still breathing. It belonged to the murderer. He'd passed out after completing his evil deeds.

This was the husband and father.

I was a professional. I had to push aside my feelings—my heartbreak over a mom who had lost everything, over girls who would never grow up to be moms themselves. My rage at the loss of innocence. My strong desire to kill the man responsible.

Another family story had ended in tragedy. Surely this man had entered marriage with high hopes, with dreams of a good life and becoming a commendable husband and dad. Yet he had literally destroyed his family with his own hands.

Violence wasn't in my family background. I had no fear of creating this kind of carnage. But I certainly felt capable of causing terrible emotional pain. I wouldn't be able to live with myself if my kids had to experience the silent darkness that I went through—that, to be honest, I was still going through. I just couldn't take that risk. I wasn't convinced that I even knew *how* to show love.

I'd never shared my childhood pain or my fears of fatherhood with Mary Jo—or anybody, for that matter. That would reveal weakness, and men are supposed to be strong and protect their families, right? I also hadn't talked about the murders of two weeks earlier. How could I expect my wife to understand my fears and feelings? It would only cause her heartache.

But now heartache was here, right in front of me. I knew my next words would devastate Mary Jo. And it seemed there was nothing I could do about it.

"Babe," I said, as gently as I could, "I was certain something inside would click and say, 'Greg, it's time to become a father.' It just hasn't happened."

Her hazel eyes welled with tears. "You lied to me. You promised we would have a family." She began to cry.

It was true. I *had* promised her. I'd thought that someday my feelings would be different, that somehow the fear would subside.

"I just—I just can't have kids right now," I said. "Maybe someday. But not now."

With tears still on her face, Mary Jo's eyelids narrowed. When she spoke, her words were ice. "You either tell me right now that we are going to have kids together or we are done."

The silence seemed to stretch longer than our marriage. She had her answer. Mary Jo turned and walked slowly down the hall and into our bedroom. Quietly, she locked the door behind her.

A YEAR LATER, I SAT alone in a sparsely furnished studio apartment and riffled through the mail. The bare walls tried to reflect light from the dim glow of the single fluorescent bulb hanging from the ceiling. I'd moved here ten months after that fateful conversation in our kitchen. Our divorce was only a month away from becoming official.

I couldn't believe that I'd lost my marriage. It had been my idea to move out. I felt betrayed, that Mary Jo had chosen kids who didn't even exist over me, that I wasn't enough for her. But I knew she felt betrayed too. Now my mood fluctuated between anger, guilt, and grief. I didn't even want to think about God's disappointment in me over the divorce.

At least I had my career to focus on. I was still firefighting. Even better, I had hope that things were going to look up. I believed that God had given me a calling.

I was nineteen when *Top Gun*, the popular movie about navy fighter pilots training in San Diego, was released. I'd dreamed of being at the controls of a plane ever since. After my air force commitment ended, I began training as a pilot and earned my fixed-wing license. Then Mary Jo and I served in Oaxaca, Mexico, on a three-week outreach trip with a Christian organization called Mission Aviation Fellowship (MAF), where I saw firsthand how missionary pilots flew in pastors, medical teams and equipment, and food and other supplies to those who needed them. From the air, some of the dirt landing strips looked like little more than walking trails. The wreckage that lined a few of the landing sites showed that there was little margin for error. Naturally, I was intrigued. After Oaxaca, I grew excited about the prospect of combining my interest in flying with missionary work. Even though one door in my life was closing, I felt the Lord was opening a new one.

I believed God was directing me to become a pilot and mechanic for MAF. I earned my private fixed-wing pilot's license and worked on qualifying for my instrument rating. I hoped that, despite the collapse of my marriage, I still had an important role to play in this world.

The only potential obstacle to my new calling was a statement I'd recently read in MAF literature that raised concerns about divorced pilots. I was certain God would work out the details, but I also wanted to clear up any uncertainty, so I wrote a letter to MAF asking for clarification. Now, as I sat in my apartment sorting my mail, I came to a letter from MAF. I held it to my chest and prayed: "Lord, I know you have called me to be a missionary pilot and I lay this in your hand. I will accept this letter as your answer to pursue this or to lay it down."

My hands shook as I slipped my finger underneath the seal and tore open the envelope. I felt that my hope and my future depended on the letter inside.

I was three-quarters through when I saw the words: "We view our pilots in the same way as ordained pastors. Unfortunately, to answer your question, we are currently not accepting applications from pilots who have gone through a divorce." I had to read it again before the meaning fully sank in.

My eyes filled with tears. I'd been wasting my time. I had no chance of fulfilling the Lord's call on my life.

I crumpled the letter and threw it across the room. *Lord, because of my divorce, I've fallen short again, haven't I? I must be such a disappointment to you.*

It seemed as if I was destined to lose everything and everyone that mattered to me. Dad had chosen to walk away when I was young. Mom had died from ovarian cancer in 1992. I'd lost my marriage. And now my dream of becoming a missionary pilot was dead.

The hopeless feeling I'd battled too often before was back.

WITH NO OTHER FULFILLING OUTLETS left, I poured all my energies into firefighting. I may have been broken as a boy, might have failed as a husband, and might be a disappointment to the Lord, but I knew I was good at my job. I figured if I became great at it, maybe God would see me in a new light.

Maybe I would too.

I expanded my training, becoming a meth-lab technician who entered drug dealers' booby-trapped houses to render safe their deadly laboratories. I was the first to volunteer to go over the side on high-angle rope rescues. I also wanted—*needed*—to be the first firefighter through the door at working structure fires.

That was the case at a house fire in the town of North Bend in December 1997. As our rig pulled up, we were met with the sound of shattering glass. Flames from the blown-out second-floor windows filled the sky. Thick smoke that reminded me of black cotton erupted from the rear of the two-story, split-level home.

I tapped my partner on the shoulder. "Mask up," I said. "We're going in."

We'd already stretched a hose up the stairs to the second-floor deck and called for water. I knelt at the door that led inside. The heat blistered the paint on the door as smoke pushed out under pressure from the frame. I put on my mask, slipped on my Nomex hood, adjusted my hose stream, flipped on my helmet flashlight, and radioed Command that we were making entry.

After our safety checks and giving my partner the thumbs-up, I kicked the door open and was hit by a blast of heat. I rolled onto my back and directed a fog stream from my hose at the ceiling of the heavily involved living room. My partner and I moved in and quickly knocked down most of the flames. I backed away until I was next to what had been floor-to-ceiling windows that lined the rear of the house. The fire had blown out the glass.

I stood. Suddenly my foot disappeared through the partially burned floor. I tried to recover my balance, but the weight of my air tank and gear pulled me backwards through one of the window openings. I fell ten feet and landed on my back, halfway down an outdoor staircase. It could have been much worse. After a trip to the emergency room, two weeks off, and six weeks of physical therapy, I was back on duty.

That would not be my last ER visit. Fifteen months later, during a night rescue of a trapped hang-glider pilot, the helicopter that arrived to extract the pilot dislodged a fallen tree from the cliff above us. The trunk struck me in the chest and sent me tumbling nearly a hundred feet down a steep embankment, injuring my back. This time I was out for ten weeks.

Despite the close calls, I had no fear. What mattered was getting the job done, saving lives and property, and showing what I could do. An incident the following year should have made me rethink my attitude.

It was a sultry August evening and I'd been assigned to Bellevue Medic 3. My partner and I had just finished a call and were headed back to the station in the medic unit, a red-and-white Chevy box van, when our pagers went off again. An elderly male was unconscious and unresponsive. I keyed the radio mic: "Fire Dispatch, Medic 3 is responding to the unconscious patient. Let's also start Engine 87 and a BLS [Basic Life Support] ambulance for transport, please."

My partner slammed the accelerator to the floor as I searched the map book for the street address. I glanced up and saw that the speedometer read sixty miles per hour. We raced north under a freeway overpass, our lights flashing and siren blaring. In the next instant, my attention was drawn to a fast-approaching intersection—and with good reason. From the east, a semitruck hauling a container loaded with apples barreled toward the intersection at fifty miles per hour, its tires locked up and smoking. We were on a collision course.

My partner yanked the steering wheel and swerved into oncoming traffic, barely avoiding a head-on collision with another vehicle. I tried to scramble into my partner's lap while still buckled in my own seat. I didn't get far. I looked to my right. The semi driver was pitched sideways in her seat, using every ounce of strength to turn the steering wheel and avoid hitting us broadside. The tractor cab began to slide sideways toward us.

Then it flipped into the air.

"Get over, get over!" I screamed.

Too late.

The semi cab and trailer landed on top of us and sent us into a slide of our own. The trailer ripped through the rear patient compartment of our medic unit. The exhaust stack of the semitruck plunged through our windshield, smashing the glass and filling our cab with exhaust. We kept sliding, off the road, until a berm of dirt finally stopped us.

Coughing, I tried to open my door, but the semi was pinned against it. Fearing that the medic unit was now on fire, I quickly disconnected my seat belt and belly-crawled through the patient compartment to the rear doors. Thank goodness, the doors still opened. Still on my belly, I crawled out the back doors and fell onto the ground. I groped at my head and body for blood and broken bones, but I seemed uninjured. Realizing that I was okay, I turned my attention to my partner. Still dazed from the impact, he signaled from his seat that he was all right.

I scrambled back into the medic unit, grabbed the aid kits, and hurried to the semi, which now rested on its side. After climbing onto the undercarriage and across the drive line, I pulled myself up to what was now the top of the cab. Stretching my arm, I reached to open the door of the semi and peered into a mess of Mountain Dew bottles and pizza boxes. The driver was there too, ghost white and scared to death, but unhurt. While lying on my belly, I extended my arm into the cab to help her out.

Though no one was injured in the accident, any or all of us could easily have been killed. For weeks after, I was plagued by dreams. In some, I faced headlights bearing down on me, accompanied by the sound of screeching tires, until I was jolted awake and found myself in a cold sweat.

I began to understand that I had chosen a dangerous profession and that I was not invincible. I could die on one of these calls. Yet even this knowledge was not enough to stop me from taking more risks and pushing myself beyond any reasonable limits. Something continued to propel me to be the best, to be the guy others viewed as capable of doing anything to help others.

In many ways I had already become that guy. The other firefighters knew from experience that when we walked into a hazardous situation, I had their back. I knew I'd earned their respect.

So why was I still unhappy?

10

BRING IT ON

Trust in the Lord with all your heart and lean not on your own
understanding.
—PROVERBS 3:5 NIV

5:35 A.M., TUESDAY, SEPTEMBER 22
KENAI PENINSULA

The smell of bacon, eggs, and coffee still lingered in camp as Matt and I prepped our packs and weapons for the boat trip upriver. For the second day in a row, a thin sheet of ice blanketed the boat deck. Using bungee cords, we quickly secured the dry bags containing extra clothing, food, a trauma kit, and survival equipment, as well as the rifle and bow cases. We each made one final scan to ensure we had all of the necessary equipment and supplies. Matt slid the boat drive selector into gear and we were under way.

The return to Doroshin Bay would be slow due to the lack of light and the threat of deadheads, the large, water-soaked logs that floated just beneath the surface of the water. Nasty things could happen very quickly if the hull was breached; too many Alaska sportsmen had lost their gear, their boat, and in some cases their lives. Matt flipped on the running lights and I moved to the bow with a flashlight. We picked our way out of the lake cove and into open water.

My anticipation was so thick that you could have cut it with a KA-BAR. I kept glancing back at my gear on the stern. For two years, that equipment and those supplies had been piled in my office, waiting for this very day. I had all the tools I needed to step into the ring with North America's largest predators. The outcome would be up to me.

Faint glimmers of light began to appear across the jagged peaks of the mountaintops, which allowed us to increase the boat speed. An hour later, Matt eased the throttle back and then killed the engine as we glided toward the shoreline of Doroshin Bay. He raised the engine out of the water, grabbed an oar and a flashlight, and moved to the bow, watching with me for anything in the water that could damage or sink the boat. I heard the familiar sound of sand and rocks scraping against the bottom of the hull. Moments later, the boat slid ashore. I looked up. The sky was absolutely clear. The temperature was thirty-nine degrees.

With our revolvers on our hips, we did a quick search for predators on the shoreline. Finding none, we offloaded the gear. The sun was in full glow along the edges of the Kenai Mountains. Shadows steadily disappeared from the ridgeline where we had spotted the bear yesterday. Matt and I sat in silence in the boat, riveted to our binoculars, inspecting every dark spot on the mountainside. After an hour of glassing and with the sun now clearly visible, Matt let his binoculars drop to his chest.

"The bear is gone."

I had to admit that he was right. Now we had a decision to make. Should we take off after the bear in hopes that we could track and find it? Or should we travel up the valley floor to conduct our original plan to hunt for moose?

From our position, it was easy to see where we'd spotted the bear on the ridgeline the day before. Once we entered the forest canopy, however, all visual references would be gone. This meant we'd have to use a compass to shoot an initial magnetic bearing and, once in the trees, continue to navigate using a compass, map, and GPS.

I didn't like those odds. "I came here to get a moose with my bow," I said. "I think we should move up a mile or so into the valley and get one."

Matt agreed. I looked closer at the trees and vegetation directly in front of us. The increasing light revealed a sight that sent a shiver up my spine. Forty yards from where the boat rested were three huge piles of scat. Matt and I walked over to check it out. Most of the scat was bright red and orange with half-digested salmon eggs. It was accompanied by huge tracks.

This scat hadn't been here yesterday. Sometime between the moment we'd left the bay the evening before and our return this morning, a bear had stood on this shoreline.

On our walk back to the boat, I reconsidered my decision to hunt with only my bow. Like any bow hunter, I wanted to travel light and with stealth, so I had already cut down the amount of gear I would haul into the field. Humping my Thompson/Center rifle would be cumbersome and tiring. I was here to match my skills as a bow hunter against one of the most sought-after game animals in the world. I didn't want to shoot a moose with a rifle; I wanted to earn it with a bow like so many men before me. And I was already armed with a revolver and bear spray.

But would that be enough to stop a black bear?

At the boat, Matt and I made a final check of our gear on the rocky shore. Did I have arrows? Did we have ammunition? Had we packed a first-aid kit? The GPS? The last thing we wanted was to backtrack over difficult terrain for a forgotten but critical item. Matt slung his backpack and rifle over his shoulders. I picked up my backpack and bow. Then, thanks to the improved light, I made another discovery— more large piles of bear scat right there on the beach.

I was sure Matt and I could handle the bear we'd spotted yesterday. Still, I was uneasy.

"You ready?" Matt asked.

"Yeah," I said. "Let's get going."

Matt started walking. I took three steps toward the wilderness, my eyes on that bear scat, then shifted my gaze to my bow and side-arm, then back to the bear scat. I glanced back at the boat and eyed my rifle case.

Yeah, I thought with a sigh, *I guess I should bring it.*

I called to Matt to wait a moment, stepped back to the boat, and unzipped my rifle case. I lifted the T/C, chambered one of the three rounds in the rifle clip, and slung the weapon onto my shoulder. From a side pocket, I grabbed three additional Win Mag rounds and shoved them into a pocket in my cargo pants. I would haul the rifle but use it only as a last resort. *Better safe than sorry,* I thought as we began picking our way up the valley.

All that morning, my mind was filled with thoughts of moose and the black bear we'd sighted the previous day. The possibility that the bear scat had been produced by a much larger and more danger-ous creature never even entered my mind.

THE WALKING WOULD HAVE BEEN difficult enough without gear on our backs, but lugging an extra thirty to forty pounds made it near impossible. In addition to the pond, we encountered frost heaves, mud pits, downed trees, and hidden holes deep enough to snap a leg in a heartbeat. Even so, we made steady progress.

On a game trail, Matt noticed fresh moose prints and scat that was still soft to the touch. I wasn't surprised. The area offered everything a moose could want: cover, food, and ample space for bedding.

We decided to sit a spell, catch our breath, and watch the openings near the tree lines. The whole area was indescribably gorgeous. The valley floor was about three-quarters of a mile across and capped on both sides by towering mountain ridgelines. The land in front of us was flat but thick with vegetation and timber. Across the valley, as far as the eye could see, muskeg moss was laid out like rolls of plush green carpet. Rising from the sea of green, towering stands of cedar, birch, and pine trees strutted their fall colors and reached toward a deep-blue Alaska sky. The only sound was a whispering wind moving through treetops. I was in awe.

I released the binoculars from my chest harness, brought them to my eyes, and scanned the valley ahead. I was so excited to be in this very spot. Each time I brought my field glasses up, I tried to will an animal to step into view.

As I searched from left to right, my eyes caught something that took a few seconds to register. I shifted my view to the left again and gasped.

"What?" Matt said.

About three-quarters of a mile away, dead center in the valley, a streak of white stood out against a brown-and-gray background. It had to be white meat on a scarred pine tree—a fresh antler rub. Moose will use trees to help them shed the felt from their antlers. This rub was clearly visible. It had removed the bark from a three-foot section of the tree.

I told Matt about the rub and guided his view to the spot.

"Oh my gosh, you're right," he said. "That's it."

I grinned. "I knew there was game in this valley. I knew it."

Finding fresh signs of moose activity was a dream come true. My hands began to shake in anticipation. Talking in whispers, Matt and I plotted our strategy. We decided to make our way along the trees at the extreme east end of the valley, to a point parallel with the antler rub. We would then traverse directly across and camouflage ourselves with pine tree branches in the vicinity of the antler rub and any game trails we might encounter. The wind was in our face, moving left to right, which ensured that if there was a bull hiding in the thickets, we wouldn't be discovered by our scent. It would be a long and methodical trek to reach that spot undetected, but we agreed that this option held the greatest potential for a successful stalk.

Everything about stalking and hunting moose is slow. If you move too fast at the wrong time, you pretty much guarantee that the moose you never even noticed standing nearby will quickly disappear, like a ninja, into dense cover. Impatience is not your friend. Many a hunter has given up after sitting motionless for six hours, only to watch a moose go crashing through the brush as soon as the hunter exposed his position.

Matt and I sprayed concentrated moose urine into the air in hopes of drawing in a bull moose. Then we slowly picked our way around mud holes, downed trees, and mosquito-infested marshes at the edge of the tree line. We focused on remaining quiet and traveling north up the valley along the tree line until we could spot the fresh antler rub. I was plenty tired from trying to keep my feet under me when Matt finally said, "There's the tree."

We rested for the next hour. It was now ten-thirty in the morning. The temperature had only climbed a few degrees. A thin layer of scattered clouds crept up the valley. Our trek had taken us longer than we'd anticipated. We guessed that even though it was late in the morning, it was still cool enough for moose to continue to feed. I knew that once the temperature rose a bit more, any moose in the area would seek the cool and protection of cover and bed down.

Matt and I spent the next hour in silence, listening, observing, and glassing every square inch of the valley. Just because we couldn't see any moose didn't mean they weren't there. Slow movement was a primary mode of protection for the Alaskan moose. I'm talking molasses-in-the-middle-of-winter slow. You could look at one spot for half an hour before catching the flick of an ear or the glint of an antler. Bam, there he was. Nothing had changed except that the dark spot you were sure was nothing had suddenly moved. I was amazed that an animal that might weigh twelve hundred pounds could hide so well.

My brother and I finally re-shouldered our packs and in a low crouch made our way to the center of the valley. The rub we'd spotted on the tree was even more magnificent than I had envisioned. You have to be a hunter to truly appreciate the excitement of discovering a fresh rub. The bark had been completely stripped away from a large portion of the tree about five feet off the ground. This had to be a big bull. Mixed within the bark at the base of the tree were clumps of blood-soaked felt shed from the bull's antlers.

I turned to Matt with an ear-to-ear grin. "This is the spot," I whispered. A series of three well-traveled game trails led to the rub. The trails were heavily marked by tracks and fresh scat left by moose and bear. Some of the scat looked just like the salmon egg–saturated waste from the shoreline. I was pleased to see evidence of both moose and bear. Maybe this day would provide the chance to fill both my moose *and* my black bear tags.

We scouted the area further, moving north along one of the game trails while trying to remain as stealthy as possible. Every couple of minutes, Matt or I would glance at each other with a big smile and nod. Everything indicated we were in the perfect location.

Once we'd surveyed the terrain, we knelt behind a small stand of willows and applied more scent control, a spray that would mask our smell, to our clothing. Then we discussed our game plan. We had come across a knoll that ran almost north–south, about fifty yards long and six feet high. A game trail that split off from one of the most heavily used trails ran south along the length of the knoll on the west side. We decided that I would set up my hide at the north end of the knoll while Matt positioned himself near the south end. When Matt started his moose calls, it ought to lure an animal off the main trail and straight to the north end of the knoll where I'd be waiting with my bow.

We synchronized our watches. I would have fifteen minutes to reach my hide before Matt started his first sequence of calls.

Matt gave me a last thumbs-up. "This is it, Greg. Be ready."

I moved one slow step after another to reach the place I'd picked out for my hide, which was between a pair of pine trees at an elevated point at the front of the knoll. Using pruning shears, I trimmed a few small branches to clear my shooting lanes. Next I found a bleached-out log partially covered with muskeg moss and dragged it into the trees so I'd have a place to sit. My field pack was to my left and my loaded rifle leaned against a log to my right. By the time I had donned the rest of my camouflage gear, placed a couple of green pine-tree branches to increase my cover, and pulled a camouflage head net over my eyes, I had only three minutes before Matt's moose calls would break the silence of the eerily quiet valley.

I still had time to arrange gear that I would use during the hunt. In front of me on the ground, I laid out binoculars, a moose call, my archery release, gloves, and a battery-powered range finder. The next step was to use the range finder to calculate the distance to various objects in my field of vision. The accuracy of the bow sight I would use to direct my arrow depended on these readings. I was proficient at hitting targets up to fifty yards out. If a moose came into view on the trail, it would be well within my kill range.

When Matt's first call rang out across the valley, I was well concealed, with camouflage covering every inch of my body. I had a perfect view of the trails in front of me and could see about one hundred yards through the trees with my binoculars. Matt's calls were so realistic that I glanced back, expecting to see a moose standing there. I envisioned the sound waves extending across the valley and up the mountainsides. My hands tingled as I focused every ounce of my energy on the trail.

Bring it on. I'm ready.

11

LOVE AND PAIN

*Wounds are what break open the soul to plant the seeds of a
deeper growth.*
—ANN VOSKAMP

In 2001, I lived with my brother Shane in a house in Lake Stevens, Washington, an hour's drive north of Seattle. From the outside, it appeared as if everything in my life was just fine. I remained dedicated to my work as a firefighter and had begun training to be a helicopter pilot. On the inside, though, I was broken. I did not want to face my disappointment and pain. It had been six years since my divorce from Mary Jo and since my dream of becoming a missionary pilot had been shattered.

I sometimes filled my Friday nights at McCabe's, a country western dance place in Everett. I didn't dance, but I liked spending time there with my brother and a buddy, Ryan, watching the girls.

On a Friday at the end of that summer, I decided to visit McCabe's on my own. A disc jockey played music for the crowd on the sawdust-covered dance floor while I tipped a longneck at the bar. Then someone tapped on my shoulder.

I turned to face two girls who looked close to my age. The "tapper" wore a white blouse, Levi's, and roper boots. She had sandy blond hair and green eyes. I realized I'd seen her there before—she was a great dancer. Now, to my surprise, she wanted a favor: "We need you to enter the Wrangler Best Butt Contest."

Apparently, she wasn't kidding.

"Nooo," I said, "I don't think so." I turned back around.

I felt another tap on my shoulder. I turned again toward the blond girl. "We really need you to do this," she said.

"No, I'm not interested."

"C'mon. It'll be fun."

As I looked closer at this persistent young woman, I realized that those green eyes were truly beautiful. An idea popped into my head.

"What's your name?" I asked.

"Rhea."

"Okay, Rhea," I said. "Here's the deal. First of all, if I do this, you're gonna do this too."

"No."

"All right, forget it." I started to turn again.

"Well . . . ," she said, "what else?"

"You have to teach me how to dance."

Rhea started talking to her friend and I thought that was the end of it. But a few moments later, she was back.

"Okay," she said. "Deal."

Both Rhea and I were forced to parade on the dance floor in front of a crowd of beer-drinking "judges." Believe it or not, both of us advanced to the next round of the best butt competition. More important, I left that night with Rhea's phone number. I called her the next day. She surprised me again with another request: Would I go with her to church?

I had not set foot in a church in a long time. Since the collapse of my marriage and my missionary dreams, I was so hurt and confused about what God was doing that I'd basically turned off that part of my life. I believed I'd let the Lord down again and felt more distant from him than ever.

The memory of those green eyes, however, was inviting me to give my faith another chance. I guess that's why I found myself standing next to Rhea the next morning in a modern church sanctuary in Everett, singing worship songs. I knew the lyrics from my days in church with Janelle. As we sang, Rhea gave me a strange look.

As soon as the service ended, Rhea said, "How did you know all the words to those songs?" She must have thought she was hanging out with a heathen.

"I've been to church a few times," I said with a laugh.

I think both of us felt something click that morning. Just seeing Rhea's enthusiasm during worship, singing and raising her hands, was infectious. I loved her magnetic smile. This was someone I wanted to get to know better.

THE PHONE WAS RINGING. IT was a Tuesday morning, just over a week after I'd met Rhea. I had fallen asleep on the couch after driving home. The caller was one of my good friends at the fire department.

"What are you doing?" he said.

"I'm trying to catch up on my sleep," I said. "We had a long shift last night."

"Are you watching TV?"

"No, I'm sleeping."

"You need to turn the news on." He hung up.

I wondered what this was about. I hit the power button for my television and was shocked to see video replays of a Boeing 767 crashing into the North Tower of the World Trade Center in New York City. Just a few minutes later, I watched live as another Boeing 767 slammed into the South Tower. Later that morning, I was horrified to see both towers collapse.

Our nation was under attack by terrorists. I couldn't believe it.

In May the previous year, at a funeral for a fellow firefighter in New York, I'd met another firefighter named Andre Fletcher, along with his twin brother, Zack. Andre was a member of Rescue 5, a unit housed at a fire station on New York's Staten Island. Andre and I hit it off immediately. Not only was Andre an FDNY (Fire Department of the City of New York) firefighter, he was also a member of one of the department's elite rescue companies. Like me, he loved the job and lived to face the danger. I spent the entire weekend with Andre, another friend, and Zack, who was also a firefighter.

On the afternoon of September 11, Zack called me. "Andre is missing," he said. Everyone from Rescue 5 who responded to the World Trade Center after the initial attacks was missing. "I need you to come out here and work on my crew," Zack said. "We need to find Andre."

I wasn't quite sure what I was agreeing to, but if a brother firefighter needed my help, no way was I going to turn him down.

I left the following Saturday, after my chief approved my time off and planes were cleared to fly again. The night before my departure, I was laying out gear in my living room and checking to make sure everything was in order, when the doorbell rang. It was Rhea. She'd put together a gift bag filled with goodies for me: a package of gummy bears, chocolate, batteries, instant cameras, a card, and a stuffed bear holding a message that said, "I'll be praying for you."

It was special that she'd taken the time to do that for me. I realized that Rhea was concerned about me. She sensed that I would be walking into a difficult situation. She was right.

The evening I arrived, Zack picked me up at LaGuardia Airport and drove me to his station near the intersection of South and Wall Streets, just blocks from the World Trade Center area. The mood was somber. The next morning, a military Humvee transported us to Ground Zero. When I climbed out and looked up, the sight was overwhelming. The towers were simply gone. Smoke still rose from the debris and rubble. The empty space was surrounded by mostly destroyed structures out of a post-apocalyptic nightmare. I didn't know how tall the closest building used to be, but it had been reduced to eight or nine stories. I could see sections where an engine from one of the jets that struck the towers had ripped open the guts of the adjacent building, leaving jagged remnants of panels, girders, and twisted steel. The image reminded me of a meat grinder. Other buildings near the towers had simply melted.

My first reaction was to turn away. *I do not want to be here,* I thought. Nevertheless, it was time to go to work. Our initial assignment was to locate pieces of the Boeing 767s that could be analyzed by investigators. We found some of those. We also found pieces of people, most commonly in the form of shoes with someone's feet still in them. Every body part was sealed inside a bag at the on-site morgue for DNA testing.

Late one day, after a week of twelve-hour shifts, I was preparing to crawl into an empty pocket of space beneath the rubble. We'd already evacuated the area twice, since portions of the "Pile," as it was known, were still collapsing. I sat for a moment on a steel I-beam, pulled my respirator from my sweaty face, and wiped dust from my eyes. When I could focus again, I noticed that amid the torn and scattered papers lying at my feet was an intact hundred-dollar bill. It was no ordinary greenback. This bill had been soaked in blood.

I couldn't help but wonder whose blood had been shed here. As I thought about it, the dam of emotions I'd been holding back since I arrived in New York finally fractured within me. I fell to my knees. Tears poured from my eyes, not just for those who'd perished but also for our bleeding nation. It sounds crazy, but in that moment I could swear I heard from deep below the skeletal, smoldering ruins of the Twin Towers the cry of three thousand entombed Americans. Their silent screams of pain were eerily and disturbingly familiar.

Without doubt, the work that my fellow firefighters and I performed at Ground Zero was important. Yet my greatest contribution during the three and a half weeks I spent in New York actually occurred right after my twelve-hour shifts on the Pile. Exhausted, covered in concrete dust, and with tools slung over our shoulders, the other firefighters and I would nod to the police officers who lined the exit path. We were crossing the threshold from one pain to another, except this pain had faces. Before us were hundreds of people holding pictures of loved ones. Some stared numbly, a hand and photo outstretched, in hopes that we would recognize the face. Others spoke through sobbing tears, calling out to ask if we'd seen their husband, daughter, grandparent, nephew, mother.

"Were you working near the South Tower? My sister was on the eighty-fifth floor and we can't find her."

"Have you seen my brother down there? Here is his photo."

A fellow first responder, Kevin Fox, and I made it our mission to spend a couple of hours each night with these hurting people. We walked into the middle of the crowd and provided an update on what we were doing. The first question after they gathered around us was always "Has anyone been pulled out alive today?" My eyes would move to the ground before I answered. I wanted to give them hope, but the words I had to speak would bring none. Instead, we gave out hugs and cried with them. When I looked into the desperate eyes of these men, women, and children, I wanted so much to bring their loved ones home. But I couldn't.

During my time there we never did find any sign of Andre or any of the eleven members of Rescue 5 who perished on September 11.

On one of my last days in the city, Kevin and I were again trying to comfort the crowds near the collapsed towers. A little girl about ten years old stood down the street. Every time I looked her way, she frantically waved at me. After nearly two hours of talking with people, Kevin and I finally made our way down the street toward the little girl. She stood in front of a large, butcher-paper mural that rested on the sidewalk against a wrought-iron fence. The mural included a man's photograph and the statements and signatures of hundreds of well-wishers.

As we walked up, the young girl smiled at us through tears.

"What an incredible mural you've made," I said.

"This is my prayer mural for my daddy to come home safe," she said. "My daddy is a fireman like you, but he hasn't come home yet."

I had to turn away. I didn't want this innocent child to see the pain that suddenly swept over my face.

Turning back to her, I said, "I believe in God. Could I write a prayer to help bring your daddy home?" She gave an excited nod. I took a felt marker from her hand and leaned over to sign the mural. I couldn't see because of the tears running down my face and onto the mural. When I looked closer, I saw the evidence of countless drops where writing had been smeared. I realized I hadn't been the only one crying while asking God for a miracle for this little girl.

I took the girl in my arms and gave her a long hug. "Your father in heaven is looking for your daddy," I said, "and will take care of him

no matter where he is." Then I said goodbye, slung my tools back onto my shoulder, and walked down the gray, dust-filled street.

AS SOON AS I GOT back to Washington, Rhea and I started spending all of our free time together. This girl seemed perfect in so many ways. The fact that she had a strong faith and was drawing me back to the Lord also felt right. I soon realized that I was in love and that I wanted to spend the rest of my life with Rhea. Amazingly, it seemed that she felt the same way.

The one dark cloud that hovered over my suddenly rising hopes was my still-present fear of failing as a father. Rhea already had a five-year-old son, Casey, from a previous relationship. Casey was great, and I knew that if Rhea and I decided to make our relationship permanent, he would be part of the package. But the idea of becoming a stepdad was more than intimidating. I was certain that at some point I would let Rhea and Casey down.

My love for both of them, however, somehow overcame my fear of blowing it yet again. I mentioned my reservations about fatherhood to Rhea but didn't reveal just how deep those feelings went. *She already has a boy*, I thought. *Maybe one child will be enough for her.*

The following spring, I bought the biggest diamond ring I could afford and proposed. Happily, Rhea said yes. Instead of planning a big wedding, we decided to elope so we could save our money for a honeymoon cruise to the Mexican Riviera. An innkeeper with a pastor's license married us on June 8, 2002, in Coeur d'Alene, Idaho. I was so thankful that after all I'd been through, the Lord had allowed love to come back into my life. I couldn't have been more thrilled.

A year later, my feelings were a bit different. I was still madly in love with Rhea. But one morning when I arrived home after a twenty-four-hour shift at the fire department, she met me in the living room.

"I've got something to tell you," she said.

"What is it?" I asked. I couldn't tell if this was good news or bad.

"Hold on," she said. Rhea left the room and returned a minute later while concealing something behind her back. I had no idea what this was about.

"I have a surprise for you," she said. Then she showed me what she'd been hiding: five test sticks from the home pregnancy kits she'd purchased at a discount store.

"Look," she said with a grin. Each one was colored blue.

I wasn't ready for news like this. "Do those even work?"

"I think so," Rhea said. "There *are* five of them."

"Oh my gosh."

It wasn't as if we'd been doing anything to prevent a pregnancy, yet I was still shocked. I just believed I was destined to never have children of my own. I was so certain I'd be a terrible dad that I didn't think God would allow it to happen.

Stepping into the role of stepdad for Casey had gone surprisingly well. I'd taught him how to fish, ride a bike, and catch a baseball. We'd gone camping as a family and we all went to church. He seemed to love all of it. Maybe I felt less pressure since I knew I wasn't Casey's biological dad. Whatever the reason, we connected.

Now, however, I was suddenly confronted with the reality of becoming a biological father—and I was terrified. All the old fears erupted like a volcano. I did not want any child to suffer with the feelings I'd been carrying with me nearly all my life, and I was so afraid of condemning a son or daughter to the same fate.

As always, though, I tried to hide my fear and pain. No way did I want Rhea to know I had such deep-seated doubts. Nor did I want to dampen her obvious excitement. Instead, I gave her a huge hug and put on my brightest smile.

But a funny thing happened over the next few weeks. As the reality of the pregnancy set in, I began to accept the idea of becoming a dad. I didn't seem to be ruining Casey. Rhea, who must have suspected my fear, kept telling me what a great father I would be. Maybe I *could* succeed at raising a family.

After a lot of thought and prayer, I decided that failure was simply not an option. I knew how to prepare for a challenge. I would train myself to become the best father I could possibly be.

To my surprise, I actually began to get excited about the baby.

It was a sunny day in August when Rhea called me at work. I immediately heard the tension in her voice. "Something's wrong," she said. "I'm bleeding and there's too much blood." At this point she was fourteen weeks along in the pregnancy.

A trip to the doctor confirmed Rhea's fears. She'd suffered a miscarriage.

Rhea was devastated—and so was I. I had actually started to embrace the idea of becoming a dad. Now that chance was suddenly gone.

I was confused and angry. *God, why did this have to happen? Why did you allow Rhea to get excited about a new baby and allow me, after all these years, to finally want to be a dad . . . and then take it all away?*

When I looked back on my life, it seemed that whenever I loved someone, any joy I felt was always canceled out by an equal measure—or more—of pain. How was I supposed to make sense of this? How could I keep living this way?

God, why?

12

ATTACK

The thief comes only to steal and kill and destroy.
—JOHN 10:10 ESV

7:45 A.M., TUESDAY, SEPTEMBER 22
KENAI PENINSULA

I sat in position at the top of the knoll, my compound bow nocked with a 175-grain broadhead arrow draped across my lap, binoculars to my face. Almost imperceptibly, I raised my view through the binoculars from the valley floor to the ridgeline above it. It was an incredible panorama: green pine trees and yellow-and-gold aspen stands stretched out beneath an azure sky. The wind was perfect, sweeping from left to right. Matt's moose calls from the other end of the knoll behind me were spot-on. I could see the game trail up to forty yards away, right where it split off from the main trail and swept toward and past me. At its closest point the trail was twenty-five yards away. Everything was in alignment. I was going to fulfill my dream of confronting a bull moose with my bow. I could not have been more excited.

There was only one problem: I'd been glassing the scene for the last three hours and hadn't spotted anything larger than a sparrow. Where was the moose? I had a pit in my stomach. I wanted to see that long-faced, four-legged creature so badly, I could barely breathe.

I thought again about why this quest meant so much to me. Yes, I longed to experience the thrill of big-game hunting for the first time, to meet the challenge of bagging a moose with bow and arrow, and to share it all with my brother. But if I was honest with myself, there was another, deeper motivation that had also led me to this moment. It had everything to do with my dad.

It had been four decades since my father left our family. I had learned how to hide the terrible wounds I'd suffered that day from others, from Dad, and even from myself. Neither Dad nor I was equipped to talk about it and neither of us wanted to go there—so we didn't. I simply pretended that the hurt didn't exist.

Yet in my mind, I was constantly replaying the conversation that Dad and I had had in the car when I joined the air force. Even though I was almost fifty years old, before every opportunity I would subconsciously ask, *Dad, will this impress you? Will this make you proud?* I didn't realize it, but the primary purpose of the moose hunt, along with so much else in my life, was to show my dad that I could fulfill the requirements of being a true man and be worthy of his love. I was on a never-ending chase for approval.

Despite this, Dad and I were close, to the point that I even thought of him like one of my best friends. He had left the California Highway Patrol and joined the Naval Criminal Investigative Service (NCIS) as a security specialist, the job he retired from after twenty-one years there. I didn't see Dad often, since he still lived in San Diego, but we talked twice a week on the phone. When I told him about the plan to hunt in Alaska, he was encouraging and supportive.

Just a week before the trip, Dad had called to check in. I was in my garage reloading rounds for the rifles Matt and I would bring. "Are you about ready?" Dad asked. "Have you got everything packed and ready to go?"

I assured him that we were almost ready. Then he let me know that he had done some research and just mailed a solar charger for our phone and GPS batteries. We had a cord that plugged into the boat, but the solar charger would give us more charging capability. *Leave it to you, Dad,* I thought, *to think of that one critical piece we can use.*

At the end of our conversation, Dad said, "Hey, double-check your list and make sure you have everything. Pay attention to all the details, just like I taught you."

I promised I would, told Dad that I loved him, and went back to work on the rounds. His words were still echoing in my mind as I measured the trim of the casings and the powder. For my rifle, I was reloading 200-grain Nosler Partition bullets. That was a big bullet, but I wanted something capable of stopping a huge animal if necessary. I was always careful, but after Dad's advice, I took extra time to make sure everything was accurate and in its proper place. If he wanted me to pay special attention to the details, that was exactly what I was going to do. These rounds would be perfect. I even added a few extra grains of gunpowder to ensure the cartridges had additional power.

Those reloaded Nosler bullets from my garage were now loaded in my rifle and resting in a pocket of my cargo pants. I hoped I wouldn't have to use them.

I fingered my bow again and thought about the shot I was preparing to make. Would the moose present me with a decent target?

Or would I have to try moving into a better position without spooking him? I felt like a sharpened spear ready to hurl myself through the air. All I needed was an objective. *Where are you?*

While training to be a pilot, I had learned to scan sections of the sky in ten-degree increments so I wouldn't miss anything. I applied this approach to my scouting through the binoculars. The scene remained unchanged, however. Thick expanses of pine trees. Stands of aspen. Heavy brush colored both green and gold. Above the vegetation, a band of shale and granite.

No moose.

With a sigh, I again shifted my binoculars to a view of the valley floor before slowly raising them to take in the trail. As before, nothing seemed out of the ordinary. Then . . .

There—to the left, thirty-five yards away on the trail. Something moved!

This was it.

I hadn't identified the source of the movement, but based on its location compared to the height of the trees, I knew it was big. It had to be a moose.

I wanted to be ready to shoot before I acquired my target, so I looked down and gently lowered the binoculars, allowing them to hang from their chest harness. I clipped my release to the bowstring, then gradually raised my head and the bow. I drew back the long graphite arrow to my cheek, peered through the bow's sights, and slowly scanned the area.

Nothing.

My heartbeat had already shifted into double time. My mouth was dry. My eyes darted back and forth, straining to detect movement. *Where is he?*

Then I saw it—only this was no moose.

At the fork in the trail, between two pine trees, stood a monster. It was over eight feet tall and six hundred pounds. It was covered in fur, dark brown with brownish-blond tips. Everything about this creature was gigantic—the thick and muscled body, the powerful forelegs and claws, the head the size of a five-gallon bucket. It was a mother grizzly, the apex predator of this country, accompanied by two nearly adult cubs, each of them close to three hundred pounds.

The mother was standing at her full height, her nose pointed high, sniffing. The other bears were on all fours, but they also had their noses in the air. Each was staring in my direction. They were hunting.

They were hunting *me*.

I felt the blood drain from my face. Sheer terror washed over me. My first instinct was to jump up and sprint for my life, but I knew that was a mistake that would end badly. I fought off the urge to run. I fixed on the mother bear's massive head, the powerful muscles in her enormous back. It wouldn't be long before she saw or smelled me. I couldn't get my mind to string two coherent thoughts together.

I felt like a child waking up from a nightmare. *Don't move the covers, don't move an inch, just close your eyes and maybe it will all go away.* Actually, that could work. I could hunker down, meld into the vegetation, and pray that I wouldn't be discovered. The bears might walk right past me.

But what about Matt?

The thought chilled me. My brother was on the other side of the knoll. He couldn't see what I was seeing. If the grizzlies moved down the trail, they'd be on top of him before he could defend himself. Matt wouldn't have a chance.

No way could I take that risk. If I stood and startled them, maybe they'd scatter into the woods. Or if I had to, maybe I could get off a couple of shots and that would be enough to discourage Mama Grizzly.

Unless all three of them charge . . . What then?

The bears were sniffing more intently. I was out of time and options. I needed to make a stand. I couldn't let them pass and get Matt.

I gently laid my bow on the ground and picked up my rifle. I dropped to one knee, raised the rifle, and peered through the scope. My hands trembled from the adrenaline surging through my veins. All I could see through the scope was brown fur—the magnification was too strong. I couldn't identify where my shot placement would be and didn't have time to adjust it.

I can't use the scope. I'll have to shoot from close range. I'll get just one shot.

I lowered the rifle, rose to a low crouch, and stepped backwards over the log I'd been sitting on. I made my way around the pine tree that hid me and moved four feet away, onto open ground. When I flipped off the rifle's safety switch, it sounded like a thunderclap in the still woods. The sow remained on her hind legs, sniffing the air, facing to her left. *If that thing charges, am I going to have the composure to aim straight and keep from firing too soon?* I leveled the rifle on my hip. To appear as large and threatening as possible, I stood on my tiptoes.

I took a deep breath and called out in the deepest monotone I could muster: "Whoa, bear!"

The grizzly's head snapped around. She dropped to all four legs. In a millisecond, her eyes shifted from round spheres to devil's slits. Her ears tucked back and the fur running the length of her spine stood straight up. A huge muscle rose from the top of her head while every muscle on her neck and back flexed into attack posture.

On four legs, the beast looked as big as a Volkswagen. She lowered her head until it was inches off the ground. She coiled, ready to spring. Her bottom lip, black as night, tightened and curled. She stared right through me.

Then, with a terrifying growl, she charged.

In my hyper-alert state I was aware of everything, as if the unfolding horror was playing out in slow motion. With each lunge of the grizzly's trunk-like legs, I observed enormous paws tear away swaths of moss and dirt that flew into the air behind her. As she barreled toward me, I heard "woofing" growls and the thud of her paws striking the ground. I felt the blood retreat from my extremities. My ears began to ring. I stood my ground, battling skyrocketing fear and a desperate urge to pull the trigger of the rifle at my hip.

Twenty-five feet.

Twenty.

My finger tightened against the trigger.

Fifteen feet. I tried to aim at the grizzly's fast-approaching head.

I squeezed the trigger.

The shot must have hit her. The grizzly didn't even slow down. The rampaging monster leapt at my face, her mouth open, exposing a black tongue and white fangs, daggers efficiently designed for their purpose: to bite, tear, and destroy.

To kill.

13

OUT OF AFRICA

Behold, children are a heritage from the Lord, the fruit of the
womb a reward.
—PSALM 127:3 ESV

Rhea and I sat in her Volkswagen Jetta. We looked at each other for a moment, then I put my arms around her and we both began to cry. We were in the parking lot of an Everett medical clinic, where Rhea had just undergone a procedure to remove the remaining tissue from the miscarriage. Any trace of our baby might now be gone, but the hurt was only just beginning.

Adding to the stress of this heartbreak was the fact that we were scheduled to fly to Africa in two days. A pastor at our church had invited me to join a missionary medical team that would teach home health practices to village leaders in Uganda for two and a half weeks. Rhea had also signed on. I would be the team EMT and Rhea would be responsible for bookkeeping and logistics.

When Rhea and I arrived home from the clinic, I went into

protect mode. "We don't have to go to Africa," I said. "I'll call the airline. Maybe we can get some of our money back."

Rhea stared at me. "So you're saying that if things get hard we're not supposed to remain faithful?" At that moment, I realized that my wife's strength and faith were greater and deeper than I'd imagined. We talked further. We both believed that God had called us to make this trip. Even though it would be difficult emotionally, we decided we needed to go.

Though we were both mourning, it helped to be in new surroundings, and in a place where we might be able to make a difference. Once we arrived in Uganda, however, I'd quickly realized that I had little to do. My primary responsibility was to simply wait and be ready to treat anyone on the medical team who might get injured. Patiently sitting and waiting were not among my gifts.

After three days of watching the rest of the team conduct training sessions, I approached Margaret Nelson, the nurse who was in charge of the program. "Is there anything *I* can teach?" I asked. She agreed to let me offer a session on first aid, provided I used only indigenous materials. It wouldn't do any good to show the villagers how to apply the splints and bandages I'd brought with me if they wouldn't have those supplies once I left. Fortunately, during two days of searching in the jungle with some of the local children, I located reasonable substitutes: T-shirts and moisture-absorbent moss to use as dressings, banana fibers to serve as bandages to secure the dressings, and branches cut from trees for splints.

The next morning, six adults and an interpreter showed up for my first training session. I taught them about the heart and the circulatory system. I traced the path a drop of blood travels through the body. Then, with Rhea acting out the part of an injured patient, I showed the villagers how to apply direct pressure to a wound with a dressing to stop the bleeding and how to elevate the wounded area.

Suddenly, my audience started talking to one another in agitated voices. "What's the matter?" I asked the interpreter. "Did I say something wrong?"

"They do not believe you," the interpreter said. "They do not believe that can happen."

"Why would they think that?" I asked.

"Because if this is true, it means that they have watched people die when they could have done something to help, but they did nothing because they did not know how."

It was sobering to hear about potentially needless deaths. At the same time, however, I was so glad that I'd spoken up and asked to teach. What I considered basic first aid was revolutionary here. It would save many lives in the future.

Once the villagers calmed down, they expressed their gratitude for the new information. Word about our class apparently spread. For my session the next morning, I had forty new and eager students.

While flying back home two weeks later, Rhea and I agreed that we'd made the right decision to keep our commitment and make the Africa trip. We'd had our hard moments, but we'd also fallen in love with the people of Uganda and contributed to making a difference in their lives. I later learned that, just days after our visit, a woman who'd attended my class used the Heimlich maneuver I'd demonstrated to save her child who was choking.

As fulfilling as that trip was, the best news was yet to come. Just two days after we returned home, I walked into the house after my first twenty-four-hour shift. I was exhausted and ready for bed. Rhea met me almost at the door.

"You're not going to believe this," she said. "Do you think after this long that my body could still give a false indication of being pregnant?"

I stared at Rhea. "Why do you ask that?"

"Well, for some reason I decided to try one of those cheap pregnancy tests again. It says that I'm pregnant. That isn't possible . . . is it?"

I didn't think so. "Did you try more than one?"

Rhea held up three blue sticks.

I wasn't about to rely on a discount test again. We immediately drove to a drugstore and bought a "real" home pregnancy test.

"There's no way," I said. "We've been bitten by mosquitoes and probably have malaria or something. We've been taking all these medications. Your body's been through too much. No way should you be able to get pregnant that fast."

Back at home, Rhea went into the bathroom and took the test. She returned a few minutes later.

"I'm pregnant."

Once again, I was stunned. "It's a miracle," I finally said. "The only way this makes sense is that we remained faithful and still went to Uganda even though we were hurting so much. God has blessed us with another baby."

This time, fear and terror weren't even part of the equation for me. I was completely on board and dove into preparations. I painted the baby's room. I bought and assembled a crib. I bought a mobile to hang from the ceiling. Even though it wouldn't be necessary for months, I secured our electrical outlets and babyproofed the house. I also read up on all the things that could go wrong medically and what could be done about them. I was going to be ready for this baby.

In November, we learned that our baby was a boy. We eventually decided to name him Benjamin, a Hebrew name which means "son of the right hand." In Hebrew, the right hand symbolizes strength. Rhea and I both liked that.

Fortunately, Rhea didn't have any complications this time around. We had a date scheduled for doctors to induce labor if contractions hadn't begun yet: May 17, 2004. Rhea hadn't had contractions when that morning arrived, but the hospital didn't have a room ready for us, so we waited. Then Rhea did start having contractions. We were both emotional wrecks by the time we finally got a room at the hospital in the late afternoon. Once a doctor induced labor, things moved fast.

Rhea and I had decided that I would be the first to hold our son. When it was nearly time for Ben to enter the world, I stood next to the doctor, watching his every move. A nurse asked if I wanted to take my shirt off and go skin to skin with Ben as soon as he was born. Of course I said yes.

I watched Ben's delivery with amazement. The doctor handed him to me and I drew him close to my chest. I even had the opportunity to cut the umbilical cord. Suddenly there I was, holding my son: Benjamin Josiah Matthews. When I gazed into his beautiful green eyes, I started bawling. It was as if there was no one else in the room. How could I have ever feared this? It was a magical moment, one I would never forget.

I don't know how long I stood there lost in a haze of wonder and joy. But it was long enough that Rhea had to work to get my attention. She cleared her throat. When I didn't react, she cleared her throat again.

"Yes?" I asked.

"Can I hold my son?" Rhea said with a smile.

"Oh," I said with a laugh. "I'm sorry. Yes, of course."

After Rhea held Ben for a few minutes, the nurse used a wash-cloth to help me give him his first bath. Even while learning how to swaddle my newborn son and change his diaper, I was still crying. I couldn't get over the idea that I now had a son.

I was not done with the delight of welcoming a newborn to our family. A little over two years later, on November 18, 2006, I cradled my baby daughter against my chest: Ciara Elizabeth Matthews. The elation and gratitude I experienced was just as strong as it had been with Ben.

Over the following months and years, it felt as if my emotions were in a fierce battle. I loved my children desperately. My ability to love had exploded and expanded beyond anything I could have imagined. I would do anything for my kids. I did not let a day go by without them hearing me say, "I love you." Every evening, I offered them a bedtime prayer and said good night with the words "I believe in you." I did not want them to ever know the pain I had endured for so long.

Despite my determination to be a great dad, however, I did not believe I would ever achieve it. Though I didn't talk about it, I was tormented by a voice inside that said that, because of me, my chil-dren were destined for a life of pain, that there was no way I could ever succeed as a dad. The conflict within me was unrelenting.

For better and worse, I remained a master at hiding my internal war from Rhea and the kids. I focused on showering them with the overpowering love I felt for each one of them. The motivation came easily—I had never known love like this before.

In those early years of fatherhood, I had no idea that this stagger-ing love for my family would one day save my life.

14

I NEED YOU TO FIGHT

When the righteous cry for help, the Lord hears and delivers
them out of all their troubles.
—PSALM 34:17 ESV

4 P.M., TUESDAY, SEPTEMBER 22

KENAI PENINSULA

The grizzly was in mid-leap, her white, razor-sharp fangs closing on my face.

My rifle shot hadn't even fazed her. There was no time to cycle the bolt and chamber another round, no time to dodge or run. My only choice was to use the rifle itself as a defensive weapon.

Leaning forward, I extended the barrel like a spear toward the bear. What I would have given to have a bayonet on the end of that rifle. With the grizzly inches away, I plunged the barrel into the bear's mouth and tried to drive it down her throat. The barrel struck something solid.

The six-hundred-pound brute smashed into me. It was like being hit by a pickup truck. At the same time, the rifle recoiled and smashed into my forehead like a blow from a baseball bat.

I was on the ground, the bear sliding over the top of me. The smell was horrendous, a mixture of rotten meat and feces that made me gag. I lay on my back and gasped for air. I tried to roll onto my side. Suddenly, two ten-inch-wide paws with extended claws slammed against my shoulders, pinning me on my back. Her upside-down face inches from mine, forelegs on my shoulders, the grizzly let out a bloodcurdling growl. I couldn't move.

The first strike of the bear's jaws came with lightning speed. My face disappeared in the bear's mouth. Three-inch canines sank deep into my neck, face, and jaws, barely missing my carotid artery. I couldn't breathe. My face erupted like a ripe pomegranate, sending a shower of blood into the air. A sudden ringing in my ears blocked out all other sound. Searing pain shot through the roof of my mouth.

I tried to scream through the bear's clenched jaws, which only served to enrage her more. The bear bit down harder. The pain was indescribable.

I can't believe this is happening.

The grizzly repositioned her bite and took the entire back of my head in her mouth. Whether from shock or the blood flowing into my eyes, I lost most of my vision along with my hearing. It was as though someone had placed a shroud over my head. I saw white light all around me, but could make out only the shadowy outline of the beast towering over me.

Without sight or hearing, I could no longer defend myself against the slashing bites being leveled against my body. I knew by the warmth on my neck that I was bleeding profusely.

The grizzly thrashed me and dragged me around like a rag doll, looking for that final moment to lunge at my neck and finish me off. When the bear released me for the second time, I snapped my head to the left and tucked my chin. I wanted to protect the gaping hole in my throat and apply what pressure I could in an attempt to slow the bleeding.

Seeing me still moving, the grizzly went into another tirade, tearing sections from my scalp and driving her teeth into my skull. I screamed again, causing the bear to once more bite harder. It felt like molten-hot brands of steel being driven into my brain.

My voice just makes her angrier. I've got to hold it in. If these were my last moments on earth, I would live them out in silence.

In a purely defensive reaction, I balled up my fist and delivered a punch to the snout of the bear. Over and over I slammed my fist into the bear's face in an attempt to get her to release my head. Yet each blow served only to increase the pressure of the bear's bite. This grizzly was determined to kill me, and my strength to defend myself was rapidly draining.

Lord, let me live or let me die, just please make it stop.

Suddenly, like the sound of a locomotive rushing by, the ability to hear roared back. Someone was sobbing uncontrollably—me. My cries had nothing to do with the pain but everything to do with the thought that I might never see my wife or kids again.

Please let me live to see my family again.

My mind had barely formed those desperate words when an overwhelming peace swept over me. It was as though God had embraced me in his arms and shielded me from the horrors of the attack. My entire world went silent again, but this time was different. It was a peaceful quiet. Then I was amazed to hear Rhea, Casey, Ben, and little Ciara calling to me. "Fight, Daddy!" my daughter said. "You have to fight to come home to us!" When I closed my eyes and listened to their voices in my mind, the memory of holding them all tight in my arms the night before I left for Alaska convinced me I couldn't give up.

The Lord's presence was as real as the predator standing over me. I sensed him assuring me that I would see my family again. As I lay on the ground, exhausted and drenched in blood, my world spinning, God spoke to me: "Greg, I love you. You are my son. I have shown you this vision of your family because I need you to fight right now."

Even in the midst of the biggest crisis of my life, I was amazed that God loved me enough to meet me in that helpless moment.

Lord, I've given everything in my power to make it out of this alive. I don't know if I have anything else. But if you're telling me to fight, I must have something left. I'll keep going till I'm unconscious or dead.

In the next instant, my sense of hearing became magnified. Though I still could not see, I was aware of every move the bear made as she circled me. In response to each thud of her paws, I rotated on my back, trying to keep my feet pointed toward the bear's shifting position. When the grizzly approached on my right side, I again used my feet and legs to spin on the ground and try to keep her from tearing into my face and neck.

My desperate movements to keep my vital areas protected signaled that the bear's tearing bites and the vicious swipes of her razor-sharp claws still had not incapacitated me. I don't know what the grizzly was thinking, but she seemed more committed than ever to finishing the terrible task she'd begun.

Somehow she outmaneuvered me—before I realized it, the grizzly was near my head again, moving in for the kill. I heard a low, sustained growl from inches above me. Hot breath blew on my face.

When the bear's paws struck my shoulders a second time, it felt like a car had landed on me. Once again, I was pinned.

I'm whipped here. In this position, there's nothing I can do. I wish I could communicate with this bear and plead for mercy, tell her how much is at stake. I don't want to lose my wife and kids!

With her fangs, the grizzly again tore into the side of my head above my left temple. I shrieked. Each time the grizzly's teeth chomped down, it felt as though someone were branding my skull with a molten-hot poker.

Where is my brother? He must have heard the shot and my screams.

I'd lost count of the number of times I'd tried to keep the bear from reaching my neck, but I was not giving up. The Lord's words echoed through my mind and heart: *I need you to fight right now.* I had nothing left. He was the one delivering the will and strength for me to keep fighting. When the Lord's words ended, they were replaced by the voices of my family crying out to me to fight.

Whenever the bear released her fangs, I felt another deluge of my own warm blood run down my head and neck. I tried to move my head away each time she lunged with snapping jaws. When I turned my head to the side, the continuous stream of blood that poured from my mouth and throat drained onto the ground and I could breathe. However, that also made my neck vulnerable to a final, fatal bite.

With the grizzly's next lunge, the entire back of my head again disappeared within her massive jaws, sending the pain to yet another level. I thought she was going to crush my skull. Though it had only enraged the bear the first time, in desperation I found myself again pounding my fists against the side of the grizzly's huge snout.

I shifted my target and was able to deliver three hard blows near the bear's ear. She must not have liked the sensation, because on the fourth punch, the jaws released their hold and then locked onto my lower right arm. With one bite and a violent head shake, she drove her fangs, still dripping with blood from my head, all the way through the flesh and muscle of my arm.

She's tearing my arm off!

The grizzly let go of my arm and turned her focus back to my head. I felt the release of weight from my shoulders as she repositioned. Quickly, I flipped onto my belly. Tucking my chin down against my chest, I tried to use my neck muscles to put pressure on the bleeding coming from the jagged, tennis ball–sized hole in my throat.

I was losing touch with my senses. Shock was setting in. My injured arm was numb. While I feared that I might lose consciousness, my mind snapped back to my EMT training. What could I do to save my own life?

As I strained to control the bleeding from my neck, I interlaced my fingers across my spine at the base of my head for protection. I knew there was no way I would survive another onslaught if I was pinned on my back. My only chance was to remain on my belly and protect my neck, face, and vital organs. I spread and locked my legs in a V to make the base of my body wider. This made it more difficult for the grizzly to flip me again. I also pointed my elbows straight out. I could use them to fight the bear's attempts to roll me over.

Twisting onto my stomach and assuming a defensive position took less than a couple of seconds. With my fingers interlaced over the top of my neck, I felt warm blood begin pouring out of my right coat sleeve and into my ear.

The bear was relentless. She wasted no time coming along my right side to choose her next point of attack. Leaning over and breathing heavily over the top of me, the grizzly reached an enormous foreleg across my back, trying to hook the left side of my rib cage with her claws and turn me over. Spreading my legs even further, I fought the force of the bear's paw. Frustrated at the failed attempt, she raised her paw above my head, claws extended.

The grizzly struck a devastating blow, dislodging my tightly clenched fingers and leaving a seven-inch gash across the back of my head. The bear's claws had ripped through my flesh starting just above the top of my left ear and extending to the base of my neck. The slash came within millimeters of hitting the vertebrae in my neck and tearing through my spinal cord. Blood poured from the wound as if from a flowing bathroom faucet. She'd sliced all the way to my skull. The sound of claw against bone was like someone running their fingernails down a chalkboard.

I'd been nearly scalped. What chance did I have now?

The sound of Ciara's voice filled my mind. She was still calling to me: "Please come home, Daddy. Fight!"

I quickly repositioned my hands to again cover the back of my neck and spine. The grizzly let out a primal "Woof!" and sunk her teeth deep into my left side, just under my armpit. With her jaws locked tight, the grizzly used her powerful neck muscles to lift me more than three feet off the ground.

I can't believe she's lifting me—she's trying to roll me over!

While hanging from the bear's jaws, I spread out both my arms and my legs to fight being flipped. Obviously infuriated that I wouldn't just die, the bear slammed me to the ground on my face. I knew she was searching my back again for another place to sink her teeth. This grizzly had certainly faced stronger and more determined victims. She was not giving up.

But neither was I. The Lord had assured me that I would see my family again, and I believed it. In my mind, I could still see Ciara calling to me. I was not going down without a fight.

My adrenaline was fading. How much more could my mind and body take? The last two minutes had felt like two hours. All that motivated me to keep fighting was the love of my wife and children and those echoing words from God that I would survive.

Why couldn't I see anything? Lord, why, at the worst possible moment, had you allowed the bear to take my eyesight? I'd lost count of the number of bites my body had endured. I knew the bear had done a number on my face and head. Had she bitten into my eyes, rendering me permanently blind? Had the grizzly torn my face off?

At that thought, despair overtook me. Would my family see me as a disfigured monster—or, worse, would I appear so hideous that they would be unable to look at me? My will to fight threatened to melt into a pool of hopelessness. I found the strength to raise my head one more time. Through a torn and bloody face, I whispered, "Please, Lord, let me see my family again."

As soon as I lay my head back down, daggers sank into my left hip. With her jaws once again locked onto my body, the bear used the strength in her hind legs to back up while dragging me sideways toward the dense brush. With each pull, the grizzly's teeth sank deeper into my hip. The pain was indescribable. I groped to take hold of anything I could to slow down our progress. Where there was nothing, I dug my fingers into the ground.

The bear stopped. I heard her move to my right side. I knew this would be my last opportunity to fight off her attack.

With adrenaline surging, I kicked blindly with my right leg, violently impacting somewhere on the bear's body. I tried to visualize where the grizzly's head was. I pulled my leg back and delivered another kick. I made contact with both blows, but neither seemed to faze the reaper circling me.

Drawing on what little strength I had left, I drew my leg back and kicked at what I guessed was the bear's face. This was my strongest strike yet, but the grizzly was ready for me. Mid-kick, she caught my leg just below the knee in her mouth and sank her fangs deep into my lower leg.

"Ahhhhhhhh!"

The pain shot straight up my spine. She must have hit a main nerve. I was in agony. I thought I was going to pass out. I knew the end was near and that my body was shutting down. My leg went lifeless in the grip of the bear's mouth. All I felt was the pressure of the bite. I no longer sensed pain. Feeling the last bit of strength drain from my body, I drew in what I fully expected to be my last breath.

Through the huffs of the grizzly's heavy breathing, I heard another sound—the shouts of a human voice.

"Whoa, bear!"

It was Matt.

15

TERROR AND TRAUMA

*Fighting terrorism is like being a goalkeeper. You can make a
hundred brilliant saves but the only shot people remember is the
one that gets past you.*
—PAUL WILKINSON

Standing up for and protecting others had always been important to me. It was part of my DNA, something I inherited from
my dad. When I was growing up, he put his personal safety at risk
each day as a highway patrolman so that he could help and protect
the public. Dad also taught me to defend my brothers if they were
ever in a jam. By the time I was an adult, the desire to shield men,
women, and children from harm was as much a part of me as my
name.

After 9/11, when I worked on the Pile at Ground Zero and heard
in my mind the screams of three thousand helpless Americans, that
desire exploded. I felt that I had personally failed our citizens and
that I had to do something about it. The drive to stop cowardly terrorists from inflicting death and suffering on an innocent population

consumed me. I would no longer settle for being a responder. Until my dying breath, I would do everything I could to stop these fanatics.

Over the next eighteen months after I returned from New York, I traveled across the country to meet with experts and attend U.S. Department of Homeland Security antiterrorism and counterterrorism courses. After some heavy lobbying, I was granted permission by my fire chief to develop and establish a new Terrorism Response Operations Division within Eastside Fire and Rescue. Our staff of ten was made up of two managers and eight new terrorism liaison officers who were trained in terrorism prevention and response. The training included how to respond to a vehicle bomb or a suicide bomber attack at a large public gathering such as a movie theater or football stadium, among other venues. We also acquired equipment and protective suits that would enable us to respond to incidents involving chemical and biological weapons such as VX, sarin, anthrax, smallpox, and phosgene. Later, I flew to London to be briefed by fire officers who had responded to the 2005 transportation bombings there, known as 7/7. I was obsessed with figuring out how to defend our country and the public from a deadly terrorist attack.

I believed the next attack would involve multiple, simultaneous, and coordinated strikes against a city or county. Managing the response to such an event and tracking down the perpetrators would require air assets. As a result, I added a commercial helicopter pilot's license to go with my fixed-wing license so I could fly both airplanes and helicopters. I began training with a local search-and-rescue organization that flew both Hueys and Hughes 500 Little Bird helicopters. That group brought me on as a copilot to assist with flying rescue missions in the mountains.

I also trained as a fugitive recovery agent. My reasoning was my belief that recovery agents are in far more homes than police officers or firefighters. While arresting those who'd skipped on their bonds, I could keep an eye out for indications of individuals who were being radicalized into homegrown violent extremists, as well as watch for signs of illicit manufacturing of homemade explosives, dangerous chemicals, or biological agents. Another reason I focused on fugitive recovery was that jails and prisons were a breeding and recruiting ground for violent Islamic radicals. I was increasing my and my colleagues' capability to identify pre-attack indicators in hopes of disrupting the next tragedy.

The training paid off in at least one instance. Firefighters responded to a residence to assist a man who was having difficulty breathing. While firefighter EMTs treated the man in respiratory distress, the company officer walked back to the medicine cabinet to try to find out what medications the man might be taking, a standard fire service practice. When the officer walked into the bathroom, he immediately noticed that the bathtub was filled with a dozen one-gallon jugs that appeared to contain urine. This officer had recently taken one of our courses and was able to immediately connect the dots. He had learned from his training that urine can be used to make urea nitrate, a homemade high explosive used in terrorist weapons. After leaving the scene, the company officer notified law enforcement about what he'd witnessed. A warrant was eventually obtained and an arrest made. The man confessed that he was indeed attempting to make explosives.

There were so many ways that terrorists or any fanatic might try to inflict harm. It was sobering and almost overwhelming to prepare for every possibility, but I was determined to try. I was on a crusade.

In 2003, two months after Rhea and I returned from Uganda, I received an email that provided a new opportunity to make a difference. It was from Margaret Nelson, the nurse in charge of the medical training program during our Uganda trip. Would I be interested in returning to Africa to develop an emergency services system for the entire country? We would teach people how to respond to a variety of crises, whether it was an accident, a natural disaster, or a terrorist attack. Margaret knew my passion for fighting terrorism in addition to my love of teaching fire and rescue skills. We both understood that East Africa was home for all manner of dangerous extremists.

Margaret didn't have to ask me twice. I saw an opportunity I was soon on a plane back to Uganda.

Over the next four years, I flew often to Africa, usually for a month at a time, and immersed myself in creating a national rescue and emergency service response system for the people of Uganda. Most of my time was spent deep in remote jungles. We established a nongovernmental organization called Samaritan Emergency Volunteer Organization (SEVO), which was funded in part by a grant that my dad helped me write. I assisted in training more than ten thousand Ugandans in bush first aid through a curriculum I developed. We established ten medical and rescue training centers across the country. We also instituted five rescue stations equipped with an ambulance, twenty bicycle EMT units, and ten motorcycle EMT units along the nation's deadliest highway. In addition, we set up rescue teams on the Ugandan border with South Sudan and the Congo to treat the hundreds of thousands of displaced people who were running from the terrorists known as the Lord's Resistance Army (LRA).

The work was not easy or always safe. On my first trip to Uganda, with Rhea, it hadn't taken long to realize that life operated a little differently there. Just after we landed at Entebbe Airport, as our plane taxied toward the terminal, we passed by an older section of the airport. I noticed that the walls of the old tower were pockmarked with bullet holes. Later, I learned that these were from shots fired by Israeli

Defense Forces commandos during their successful rescue of hostages held by terrorists in 1976.

Then, just after we'd landed, we stopped at a market so two members of our team could buy water and malaria medication. An agitated man walked up to our van and threatened us with a huge bowie knife. Everyone in the van was terrified. While David, our guide and driver, got out and talked to the man, I quietly slid open the van door, ready to respond if the situation turned violent. Fortunately, after David gave the man a small amount of money, the would-be attacker put his knife away and walked on.

I was relieved but also unnerved. *My gosh,* I thought, *we've been on the ground only thirty minutes and we've already been threatened by a man wielding a knife. Is this how it's going to be?*

Sadly, intimidation and violence were a regular part of life for many in Uganda. For nearly two decades, the LRA had terrorized people in the northern region of the country. LRA tactics included mass atrocities and the kidnapping of children; some kids were forced to shoot their parents and then join the rebel army. Thousands of Ugandans fled their homes to escape the fighting between the LRA and government troops. According to one estimate, nearly two million people resided in temporary IDP (internally displaced persons) camps because of the conflict.

During one of my absences from Uganda, our organization established medical teams to serve the people in the camps. On my next trip to Africa, I was invited to view their work in person. An American embassy official recommended I stay out of the north—he showed me a picture of a missionary and his wife who had been murdered there. I knew that a Caucasian male could be an obvious target in that area, but I decided I needed to go. Though I saw plenty of evidence of the fight between the government and the LRA, including armed patrols, I fortunately avoided any incidents. Even so, it was unsettling to witness some of the traumas that our team was treating, such as machete and gunshot wounds. Evil forces were definitely at work here.

As bad as it was in the north, a sense of lawlessness could be found almost anywhere in Uganda. Motor vehicle accidents were frequent, since roads were terrible, there was no lighting, and people drove too fast. When an accident did occur, what Americans would consider normal emergency procedures and behavior did not apply. For many Ugandans, for example, a highway death was an opportunity to loot. Some might even steal a dead person's shoes, because the deceased wouldn't need them anymore.

Part of the early training I conducted with SEVO volunteers was on how to respond to a road accident. Since flares were unavailable, I taught the volunteers to build a fire to warn approaching motorists that there was an accident ahead and indicate they should slow down. One day what was called a taxi—actually a Volkswagen bus, filled with more than a dozen people—collided head-on with another vehicle on the pothole-marked highway. Some of the passengers were killed instantly, while others were badly injured.

Our team of SEVO volunteers responded to the injured and built fires at both ends of the road. Then a large commuter bus approached the scene at fifty miles per hour. The driver saw the warning fire but decided that the volunteers were trying to slow him down in order to rob him, another common trouble in Uganda. Instead of slowing, the driver accelerated and raced through the accident scene. He struck and killed eighteen people, including three SEVO members. It was a terrible reminder of the challenges we faced.

Because of the threats posed by LRA terrorists and even Ugandan citizens, security was another vital part of my work in the country. I performed security risk assessments of our rescue stations and made sure we had secure places to lock up vital medical equipment and supplies. I also helped build relationships with the national police in the towns where we established rescue stations so they would protect our SEVO responders when an incident occurred.

Most of Uganda's problems were man-made, but natural ones could be just as dangerous. One night, during a party in the jungle to celebrate a wealthy man's donation of land to SEVO, I decided to get away from the festivities for a few minutes and take a hike with a security specialist and a SEVO member. The three of us were walking down a trail surrounded by thick vegetation, me in front, when we heard a tree branch snap to our left. Each of us turned in that direction, our headlamps illuminating the area. On the ground between two trees, about forty feet away, a pair of huge, yellow, catlike eyes stared in our direction.

"Don't move," said the SEVO man behind me. "That's a leopard."

I stopped breathing. Suddenly I wished I'd stayed at the party.

"Let's walk slowly backwards," the SEVO man said.

We did. Our headlamps stayed fixed on those unblinking yellow eyes, which watched our every step with laser-like intensity. When we felt we'd retreated far enough, caution was no longer needed—we turned and ran as fast as we could back to the camp. If the leopard gave chase, we were moving too quickly to notice.

TRAVELING TO AFRICA FOR MORE than two months a year was sometimes hard on my family. It was especially tough on Rhea. When I returned home from a Uganda trip, I usually spent a couple of days with my wife before going back to work at the firehouse. We needed time to reconnect and share what was going on in our lives.

During those first days at home, I often found myself up late at the computer in my office, looking up antiterrorism employment opportunities across the country. I knew I was doing good work at home and in Uganda, but I needed to do more to protect my country and prevent terrorism. My goal was to serve a metropolitan city that was a likely terrorist target and be responsible for protecting a large population of American citizens. One night, as I scrolled through various job openings, my heart skipped a beat—the city of San Diego was seeking someone qualified to fill the roles of both a homeland security manager and an emergency manager.

San Diego was home. This was perfect. I applied immediately.

It took months of deliberations, background checks, a polygraph test, and multiple interviews, but I was eventually blessed to be offered the position. Rhea was originally from California, so she was all for the move. I woke up every morning having to pinch myself that the Lord had given me such a huge opportunity and responsibility.

The new job meant having to put an end to my work in Uganda, however. I knew I would leave SEVO in capable hands—Hannington Sserugga was one of the six men who had attended my initial first aid class and was dedicated to helping his people. When we formed SEVO, he served as director in my absence. The other board members were also dedicated. For me, seeing what we'd accomplished was like looking at a plowed, furrowed field. The seeds had been planted and watered. The soil had been tended and weeded. Now we were watching the sprouts begin to come up. My work here was done. Hannington and the rest of the team would grow the program to new heights and make it truly Ugandan.

Even so, it was hard to say goodbye. My last trip to Uganda was in July 2007. After I'd officially turned over my responsibilities and equipment and signed the necessary documents, fifty or so people accompanied me to Entebbe Airport. We gathered in the airport parking lot. As always, the Ugandans called me "grandfather," a sign of respect. I received many hugs and witnessed many tears.

"Uganda will always remember what you have done for her and us," Hannington said. "Many lives have been saved in many ways. You brought something to Uganda that we never would have had otherwise. We will never forget you."

The strange thing is that despite the heartfelt words, I would not allow myself to step back mentally and take any credit for my four years of efforts in Africa. I felt little satisfaction. Even as my colleagues and friends gathered around to thank me and wish me well, only half of me was with them. The other half was already thinking about my new position in San Diego and what I needed to do.

Despite my growing influence and impact in the realm of anti-terrorism, I was not at peace. On my way to visit the IDP camps in northern Uganda, I'd ridden in the back of a flatbed truck for eight hours. I should have been mentally preparing for what I would do if we were unexpectedly attacked or been rehearsing how I might encourage our SEVO volunteers at the camps. Instead, all I could think about was my kids. My dad had missed so many events that were important to me as I grew up. Because of my travels, I'd also missed too many of Casey, Ben, and Ciara's plays, baseball games, and school open houses. I pictured each of them as an adult, standing and smiling in a roomful of people, but on the inside feeling alone and in pain because their father never gave enough, leaving them feeling unloved.

Nobody told me I was failing, but I couldn't shake the feeling that I was letting everyone down: my kids, my wife, my dad, and God.

No matter what I did, I heard the same message over and over in my mind: *You will never be a good dad.* I saw only one way to overcome this and earn the respect and love of my family and the people around me. I needed to take my efforts to the next level. I needed to do more.

16

I THINK I'M DYING

We shall draw from the heart of suffering itself the means of inspiration and survival.
—WINSTON CHURCHILL

4:08 P.M., TUESDAY, SEPTEMBER 22

KENAI PENINSULA

"WHOA, BEAR! WHOA, BEAR!"

Matt yelled at the grizzly at the top of his lungs. The bear reeled in my brother's direction, my leg still dangling from her jaws, to size up this new threat. I still had no vision, but I could hear and feel Matt and the grizzly's steps as the three of us twirled in a bizarre dance of death.

The beast was directly between us. The trees were too thick along both sides of the narrow trail for Matt to change position and take a clean shot with his rifle. If he fired from where he was, the Nosler slug would surely travel through the bear and hit me. So, to distract her,

Matt repeatedly charged toward the grizzly and yelled, then quickly backpedaled.

With each advance, Matt moved a little closer to the bear. He definitely had her attention, but she wasn't moving and she wasn't letting go of me.

Finally, Matt ran even closer, within twenty-five feet. The giant sow lowered her head and locked black pupils on Matt's. It was like staring into the eyes of the devil. My brother hesitated only an instant, then took one more step.

That did it. The grizzly released my leg. She dropped her head further and emitted a deep, guttural growl. The bear curled her lower lip. The hair on her back stood up. When she bared her fangs, blood—my blood—dripped to the ground.

I was in helpless agony. There was nothing I could do.

Matt stepped quickly to his left, trying to put me out of the line of fire.

The grizzly charged.

Matt raised his rifle to his shoulder and fired. Flames leapt from the end of the barrel, briefly obscuring his view. The bullet caught the rampaging monster in the left shoulder. She kept coming.

Matt cycled the rifle bolt back, ejecting the spent cartridge. He slammed the bolt forward, chambering another round.

At the same instant, the bear braced her front legs, slid to a stop ten feet from Matt, and reared onto her hind legs. She towered two feet above my brother, roared, and stepped closer. Suddenly she lunged, jaws open. She was going for Matt's head.

My brother fired again.

The second bullet struck the behemoth in the upper part of her neck. Either Matt had hit a sensitive area or the combined effect of the wounds had registered. Either way, the grizzly suddenly dropped onto all fours, turned to Matt's left, and bolted off the trail into thick vegetation, snapping trees like matchsticks as it ran.

Matt stood in place, his body shaking, shocked by what had just happened. I was on my hands and knees, blood pouring from my wounds. The grizzly was not gone. Matt couldn't see the bear, but we heard her growling and pacing about thirty yards away. Had she had enough or was she gathering strength for another attack?

Matt watched the trees in the direction of the growls, his rifle raised. A minute passed. Two minutes. Matt finally rushed over, knelt beside me, and placed his hand on my back. "Greg, we've got to get out of here," he said. "That bear's still alive and I'm not convinced she's not coming back."

I couldn't see, but I could hear my blood dripping into pools below me from the lacerations on my neck, head, and face. Blood and saliva also poured from my mouth where the grizzly had driven a fang through my left cheek and jaw. With my tongue, I felt the dime-sized hole. I didn't believe any of this. *There's no way I was just attacked by a grizzly.*

"Greg," Matt said again, "we've got to get you out of here!"

I was so exhausted. Waves of nausea and shock washed over me. My head spun. I avoided turning toward Matt, because I just knew he would tell me my face was gone. My face and mouth had suffered so much trauma that I could barely speak.

"Matt," I rasped, "I think I'm dying."

"No, you are not dying!" Matt snapped. "Tell me what to do, Greg. Tell me what to do."

Matt's words echoed in my brain as if he were speaking from the other end of a long tunnel. I shook my head to try to clear the confusion. *Think, Greg, think.* Nothing was making sense.

Then a remnant of my EMT training kicked in. *I've lost a lot of blood. I'm going into shock. We've got to control the bleeding—now.*

"I can't see anything," I said. "You need to be my eyes and hands. I'm going to rise up on my knees. You get in front of me and tell me what you see."

I drew in a long breath, spit out a chunk of coagulated blood, and slowly straightened up. The drop in blood pressure brought on a fresh wave of nausea.

"Your cheek has been torn away from your upper lip," Matt said. "You have a deep, two-inch laceration that extends down the center of your forehead. You have—"

"What about my face? Did it get my eyes?"

"There's a lot of blood but it looks like your eyes are fine," Matt said. "Your face, it's serious, but I'm sure it's repairable." He paused a moment. "Though I will say it looks like I'm moving to the top of the list as most handsome sibling."

I tried to laugh. At least Matt still had a sense of humor.

"I'm most worried about the bite to my neck," I said. I slowly raised my chin.

Matt gasped. "Oh my God," he said. "It's deep and bleeding badly. The wound starts above your jawline and goes down across your upper neck. It's open and the flesh of your neck is just hanging down. You're losing a lot of blood from there."

I asked Matt to find me my shemagh, a Special Forces scarf I'd been wearing. Seconds later, he placed it in my hands. I spun it into a narrow, flat bandage and pressed it against the hole in my neck.

"Matt, I need you to come over, grab both ends of the scarf, and tie it tight over the top of my head. I'll tell you how tight to make it so it doesn't completely cut off my blood supply."

Matt tied the scarf with half a knot on the side of my head. "Tighter, Matt. It has to be tighter." My brother pulled back on both ends of the scarf and tied a perfect square knot. I felt the bandage. It was soaked in blood, but I knew from experience it would stay. After I gave Matt more instructions, he spent the next five minutes applying heavy, direct pressure to my neck to keep me from bleeding out.

Matt moved behind me to assess the back of my head and neck where the grizzly had buried her claws. I knew the sight would be ugly. In my head, I could still hear the sound of those claws scraping against my skull as if she were sharpening them against a tree trunk. My brother said the wound was about seven inches long, starting at the top of my left ear and ranging down across the back of my neck to my spine.

"Can you see the bones of my spine?" I asked.

"No. But the entire back of your head has been scalped and it's bleeding really bad."

My nausea was increasing. Trying to stay upright on my knees was becoming more and more difficult.

I suddenly remembered that Matt had also been wearing a shemagh. I asked him for it and spun it into another bandage, wider than the first so it could cover the back half of my head. While Matt continued to apply pressure to the gaping wound in my throat, I worked to control the bleeding at the back of my head and neck. With Matt's help, we got it tied, again with the right amount of pressure.

Exhausted, I fell forward onto my hands. I felt as if I'd just run a double marathon. Another wave of nausea hit me but I managed only a single dry heave. The world spun. All I wanted was to lie down, just for a moment.

"Greg," Matt shouted, "we have to get out of here!" The words were muffled, as if my brother were talking to me from underwater.

I realized that my shock was deepening. When I worked on trauma patients who were severely injured and they looked up at me with that thousand-yard stare, I'd often wondered what they were feeling and thinking as they slowly slipped closer to death. Now I knew: they just wanted to rest. At those moments, I knew there was no stopping the progression of shock when it passed a certain point. Once my patients crossed the line, my efforts to keep them talking to me accomplished nothing. What they needed was the return of oxygenated blood to the brain, heart, and lungs.

Now it was my turn. I was going into irreversible shock. Now I was the one who needed oxygenated blood, who was unable to speak intelligently, staring into space with lifeless eyes.

The Big Lie was whispering to me. It was trying to convince the depleted muscles in my arms and legs to just relax and let my body fall to the ground. Deep inside, I knew I couldn't do that. The last thing I could afford to do was delay moving toward the boat for help. Yet the fatigue and temptation were overwhelming.

Surely, my mind insisted, *I can just lie down for a second and regain my strength to walk out of here.*

It was my last thought before I passed out.

AT THAT MOMENT, MORE THAN three thousand miles away, my wife, Ben, and Ciara were just finishing dinner at a family friend's home in Plano. I'll let Rhea tell the story.

Mari and her husband, Tim, and their kids were some of the first friends we made when we moved to Texas. They had a son the same age as Ben and a daughter the same age as Ciara. Mari and I instantly became very good friends. Mari had invited us over for dinner on September 22. As usual, we had homemade Mexican food:

tacos, chilaquiles, chips, and Mari's special hot salsa. The whole meal was amazing.

Like always, we were having a wonderful visit. But this night I was a little uneasy. It had to do with Greg—which was odd, because I was used to him leaving. When he was going to Africa, he'd be gone for a month at a time, so this hunting trip was nothing unusual. But I'd started to get this strange feeling the last week or two before he left. He was working on his medical trauma kit. Then we had the conversation about the bear spray. He and Matt were talking on the phone all the time—they were over-the-top with preparing for this trip. And little by little I was realizing that this hunt really could be dangerous. Greg was even practicing his moose calls in our backyard every day. I thought, Okay, what other animals will that sound draw in?

At the time, my son Casey was in college in Nevada. During those last days before Greg left, my uneasiness got to the point where I even asked Casey on the phone, "Do you know where we keep our life insurance stuff? Do you have a house key? Do you know our neighbors' phone number? Would you know what to do if something were to happen to me and your dad?" He didn't want to talk about it.

It wasn't an overwhelming concern. I wasn't panicked. It was just what I call a check in my spirit.

At Mari's house, after dinner, she and I sat down with a glass of wine in her small front living room while the kids played either upstairs or on the trampoline in the backyard. The living room had hardwood floors and a picture window with a view of the front yard. I had my feet up on the couch. I should have been totally relaxed, yet I was still troubled.

Mari asked about Greg and the trip. I told her what I knew.

Then I added, "Just keep him in your prayers. I have this weird feeling."

"Really?" Mari asked. "Why? He hunts all the time, doesn't he?"

"Yeah, he does," I said. "But this is different. This is Alaska. I just feel weird about it. A little worried. I don't really know why. Just keep him in your prayers."

"GREG. GREG!"

Matt was shaking me. I was lying on my side. Fear gripped me when I realized I'd passed out.

I opened my eyes to an amazing surprise—my sight had returned. I was also astonished to realize that my nausea had diminished. I still had a chance to survive this nightmare. But I had to get up.

Crushing pain was shooting through my right arm. When I looked down, I understood why. My arm was deformed, as if someone had laid it on a table and taken a sledgehammer to it. A steady stream of blood flowed from the sleeve of my jacket onto the ground. It was the first time I'd seen any of my injuries.

I have a weird relationship with blood. I can watch other people lose blood all day long and not be affected. But when it's *my* blood, the story is entirely different. I was actually banned from giving blood, because as soon as I see that dark fluid filling the little clear bag, I begin sweating and my face turns ashen. Pretty soon, nurses are running around, looking for a paper bag for me to breathe in. So much for being a tough fireman.

Now, however, the only thought that came as I watched blood pour out of my sleeve was that the human body can lose only so much before reaching the point of no return.

I have to get up. I have to get up. I have to get up. My mind kept repeating the message but my body wasn't cooperating. I was too wracked by exhaustion and pain.

Then I heard a voice in my head, as crisp as the icy wind whipping through the treetops above us: "It's not over yet, Greg. I need you to get up and fight."

God was speaking to me again.

Images of Rhea and the kids flooded my mind. If I lay there much longer, I would die. I rolled from my side to my belly and tried not to look at the pool of blood beneath me. Forcing my hands and injured arm under my chest, I pushed as I hard as I could and rose to my hands and knees.

Matt still knelt beside me, his eyes on the tree line, anticipating an explosion of branches and a second charge of the grizzly. We quietly discussed our exit strategy. My brother said that as we walked, he would use one arm to assist me and hold his rifle with the other.

I spotted my rifle on the ground. The barrel and scope were still wet with blood. After doing our homework on past hunting tragedies, Matt and I had decided to use the same ammunition, reducing the chance of running out in a desperate situation. This was a desperate situation.

"Matt, there's still ammo in my rifle," I said. He grabbed my rifle, cycled the bolt, and reached in to pull the remaining two rounds from my clip.

"We've got to go, Greg. I'll help you walk. I'll keep my eyes on our back trail in case any of those bears decide to come back."

Still on my hands and knees, I turned to look up at my brother. His widened eyes told me he was just as scared as I was.

"I think I can walk on my own if I can just get to my feet," I said.

"You can do this, Greg." Matt reached under my left armpit and helped me up. My legs were like rubber bands. I felt my blood pressure drop. The dizziness returned with a vengeance.

I looked down. My right lower pant leg was drenched in blood, along with my boot. The right sleeve of my jacket was a deep crimson, blood running out of the holes in the material. Both my shoulders and the front of my jacket were saturated in bright red fluid that was dripping onto my legs. I was a mess.

Seeing that river of blood run down my jacket must have been too much. My head spun and a dark gray ring closed in on my vision. My legs nearly buckled as surges of shock pelted me. I knew that from this point shock would be the predator seeking to take my life. When a person suffers severe trauma, different types of shock can set in, affecting both the brain and body. Psychogenic shock, caused by fear, can render a person incapable of functioning physically or mentally. The blood vessels dilate so that oxygen-rich blood no longer circulates to the brain and heart. Hypovolemic shock has the same effects but is far more dangerous. It's caused by a loss of blood outside the body and holes in the circulatory system. Once it takes hold, it is often irreversible. I would potentially confront both of these types of shock during my desperate escape.

Common sense can be a blessing or a curse, depending on the situation. We were a mile and a half from the lake and our boat. When I looked across the valley at the never-ending sea of obstacles that stood between me and safety, I thought, *What man in his right mind would paint himself with blood so he smelled like a fresh-cut rib-eye steak and then proceed to walk more than a mile across both wolf and grizzly country?*

To take that first step in the direction of safety, I bargained with myself. *Start walking, Greg, one step at a time. You can always quit and give up.* Once I made that deal with the voice in my head, I was able to move and keep my eyes on the prize—surviving.

I took the lead, blanketed with fear, and slowly began retracing our zigzag path across the swampy valley. When I moved into an area of smaller timber, an ice-cold Alaska wind blew through my blood-soaked jacket, chilling me to my weary bones.

"You can do this, Greg," Matt called from behind. "I know you can do this."

I picked my way through a tangle of brush, tightly grouped willows, downed trees, and holes filled with mud that could suck a boot right off your foot. I turned to look at Matt. He was ten feet behind me, walking almost backwards, rifle held with both hands, tense eyes fixed on the trees in our rear. When I glanced down, I understood his concern exactly. I was leaving a steady trail of blood on the ground and smeared on every branch and limb I came in contact with. If the grizzly was stalking us, she would easily discover the blood-soaked trail and soon our exact location. Like a warship traveling at night through enemy waters, lights turned on and radar pinging, we would be hard to miss.

The marshy terrain had been difficult enough to traverse when we crossed it in the morning. In my current state, it seemed impossible. Frost heaves hid holes as deep as three feet, while tall grass and brush required high stepping that drained precious energy from my legs.

My body and mind were at war with each other. My body screamed, *Just take a break, Greg! Stop and rest, if only for a second. Just stop, lie down, and catch your breath.* A steady stream of lies bombarded my determination to take another step. Then the enemy voice went for the jugular: *There's no one at the boat and no one within miles that can help you. No matter what you do, you'll end up tired, cold, and dead. Just give up and rest.*

Yet some part of my mind knew my exhausted body was trying to kill me. I spoke out loud against my body: "No! I can't stop or I may never get out of here alive."

I thought I was going crazy. I tried to ignore the voices in my head and focus on mustering the strength for another step. But I was moving slower. Instead of looking up to catch sight of the boat in the distance, I started looking down for a place to collapse. Yet, each time my eyes identified a potential resting spot, something prevented me from stopping. Sometimes it was a vision of the smiles and outstretched arms of Rhea and the kids. They begged me to keep moving: "Daddy, if you stop, you can't come home." Other times, at the exact moment when I was ready to bend my knees and raise my arms to brace my fall, I felt the Lord's quiet whisper. It was the same message he'd given me earlier: "I need you to fight, Greg. I am not done with you." It encouraged me to keep going just a little longer.

We were probably halfway to the boat when I confronted a huge downed tree, gray from many seasons of exposure, that had fallen across the path. To me it looked like the Great Wall of China. To go around it would mean venturing deep into the unforgiving swamp. I'd never make it. The only other option was to break several limbs loose so I could climb over it.

After all I've been through, Lord, can't you just make it easy? What does a man have to do to live around here? I stepped up to the horizontal tree trunk. My body shouted for joy over the brief relief of being able to lean against something. I put both hands against the top of the tree trunk, raised my right leg, and struck hard at the bases of the limbs that blocked my path. The tree had been dead for a while, so my feeble attempts to snap off the limbs met little resistance. I threw my right leg over the tree, lifted myself up, and straddled it like a horse.

Unfortunately, I didn't have the strength to stop my momentum. I fell over the top of the tree and crashed to the ground on the other side in a heap of awkwardly bent limbs and blood. On my hands and knees in the mud, I began to cry out—not from the pain, not from exhaustion, but from the swell of emotions that suddenly pounded at me like a hurricane against a jagged shore.

I had reached my end point. The voices in my head fell silent. I did a slow roll onto my side and closed my eyes. I was not getting up again, and the scary part was I was fine with that.

Matt screamed from behind me, asking if I was okay, but I made no effort to respond. He scrambled quickly over the downed tree and found me lying on my side.

My brother again knelt next to me. Lying on the ground, in shock, confused, and nearing hypothermia, I lowered my head to the ground and spoke in a barely audible voice.

"This is it, Matt. I can't make it."

17

DREAM JOB

Security is a process, not a product.
—BRUCE SCHNEIER

To a guy who's never much appreciated rain or being cold, August in San Diego is just about perfect. The average yearly high is seventy-seven degrees and the average low is sixty-seven. A walk through downtown while relishing the heat of the sun on your face and the spectacular view of the harbor and Pacific Ocean is one of life's joys.

When I started my job as a homeland security manager near the end of August 2007, however, I was feeling the heat in more ways than one. I was one of eight managers in the city's Office of Homeland Security. My specialties were antiterrorism, emergency management, and emergency planning. Along with the other managers, I was charged with allocating more than $18 million in federal funds toward city and county agencies. I had traded my firefighting duties for being responsible for protecting more than a million San Diego residents from terrorists.

The transition from my old career to the new was dramatic. Although I had introduced new antiterrorism programs at Eastside Fire and Rescue, I was primarily a firefighter and EMT, all about operations and hands-on work. Now virtually all of my time was devoted to leadership and administration. Instead of a helmet and turnouts, my new uniform was a sport jacket and tie.

That first week, when each morning I parked my car beneath the ironically named World Trade Center, waved at the security guard, and rode an elevator to my office on the tenth floor, I wondered if I'd bitten off more than I could chew. Was I truly capable of fulfilling this assignment? Could I keep an entire city from harm? San Diego was a hotbed for terrorists. Three of the 9/11 suicide hijackers had lived in the city and other hijackers visited them here. Two took flying lessons in the area. San Ysidro, at San Diego's southern boundary, was likely the busiest land border crossing to another country in the world. San Diego's western border included America's largest concentration of U.S. naval war assets.

Then there was Anwar al-Awlaki, an American-born Muslim cleric and high-ranking al-Qaeda operative. While living in San Diego, al-Awlaki had mentored the hijackers during their time of flight training. Not only did al-Awlaki act as a cell handler in San Diego for 9/11 operatives, he also radicalized U.S. Army major Nidal Hasan, who would fatally shoot thirteen people at Fort Hood in 2009. Though al-Awlaki had fled the area after 9/11, he continued to produce online videos encouraging extremists to attack the United States. The mosque where al-Awlaki served as imam was near my home in El Cajon—my work had brought me full circle.

For terrorists, San Diego was a target-rich environment. I was deeply concerned that, in a sea of hidden threats, I would miss something. In terms of my career, the burden of my duty was heavier than any I'd carried before. My days were filled with managing programs and schedules, filling out budgets, answering emails, and coordinating meetings and teleconferences. I came home mentally drained. Often, if I sat down on the couch, I was out in minutes and done for the evening.

I was a bit like the Bible's David, a shepherd who had somehow been promoted to the position of king, only I didn't feel I belonged and didn't know what to do next. I was too overwhelmed to succeed on my own. I decided I needed extra help. My day started at seven-thirty each morning, but on one of my first days on the job, I got up early and arrived at the World Trade Center at six-thirty. After stopping at my office, I carried a cup of coffee down a hallway, opened a door, and stepped onto the gray steel slats of a fire escape.

The sun was just beginning to peek over the tops of the highrises around me and would soon deliver fresh summer sweat to the asphalt and pavement below. My "private suite" had a partial view of San Diego Harbor's brilliant blue to the southwest, but I wasn't here to enjoy the scenery. I set down my coffee and gripped the railing in front of me.

"Lord," I said, "please forgive me of my sins. Don't let my sins stand in the way of you executing your safety and protection over these people. I know that I asked for this opportunity and you delivered, but I'm a little intimidated by this position. I need your presence and guidance."

I raised a hand, extended it toward one area of the city after another, and asked God to prevent evil from having any influence there. I finished my prayer time by saying, "Lord, I know I have the background and training, but I need your wisdom to make the right decisions and connect with the right people. Allow me to build those networks that will bring people together so that we can keep San Diego safe from terrorists."

This felt right. My fire escape meetings with God became a regular part of my routine. They drew me closer to him and seemed to give me the energy and focus I needed to face each day.

Just a few weeks later, I would need that energy and focus. On October 21, shortly after noon, arcing power lines whipped by Santa Ana winds ignited a small fire northeast of San Diego, near a stream known as Witch Creek. That same day, what would be named the Harris Fire ignited to the south, near the border with Mexico. Dry and gusty winds quickly blew these and other small fires into conflagrations, all headed toward San Diego. By four o'clock the next morning, the Witch Creek Fire had reached the city limits. We were suddenly dealing with multiple firestorms.

Because of my emergency management experience, I was assigned to the city's Emergency Operations Center (EOC) in the basement of an administration building. The center consisted of a huge room with four-by-six flat screens filling one wall and a series of tables arranged in the shape of a U. Two desks sat at the opening of the U, which were the workstations for the director of homeland security and my boss, the deputy director.

The challenge of responding to the growing crisis was enormous. We had to coordinate the actions of firefighters; the overall city, county, federal, and Red Cross response; and the evacuation of hundreds of thousands of people. Some citizens didn't make it. In those first days, a fifty-two-year-old man refused to leave his Tecate home when the area was threatened by the Harris Fire and ordered evacuated. His charred body was found a couple of days later. Seventeen people would eventually lose their lives due to the fires.

On October 23, I was at my desk in the "U" at the EOC when I heard my boss talking on the phone. She had just learned that the director was coordinating an off-site evacuation, leaving her in charge at the EOC. Now she was answering phones and trying to deal with a thousand details. "Where," she said in a frustrated voice, "are we supposed to find ten thousand cots?"

I was a planning section chief. I also knew I was probably one of the few people in the room who had real-world experience with the incident command system, a national model developed in the late sixties and seventies for managing a large-scale emergency involving multiple agencies and jurisdictions. I walked over to my boss's desk.

"Could you use some help up here?" I asked.

"Yes," she said. "We need to set up a mega-shelter at Qualcomm Stadium [then home of the National Football League's Chargers] for potentially a hundred thousand evacuees. I need to write some objectives."

"Well," I said, "let's make sure we write SMART objectives."

"Smart? What do you mean?"

"Specific, measurable, action-oriented, realistic, and with a time element," I said. "SMART."

"Show me what you're talking about."

Over the next twenty minutes, the director and I came up with a series of objectives that we posted and began assigning to various team members. For the rest of the wildland fire crisis, whenever I was on shift, my assignment was deputy director of the EOC. In what was literally a trial by fire, it seemed I passed my first test in emergency response with the Office of Homeland Security.

At the height of the crisis, San Diego's fire and rescue department deployed 73 engines, 7 trucks, and 420 people. Along with managing the emergency response, we coordinated the delivery of

city supplies—trucks filled with blankets, pillows, water, and more—
to evacuees at Qualcomm Stadium, until federal supply deliveries
kicked in. We even established an emergency veterinary and medical
care shelter for large animals on nearby Fiesta Island. By the time
the fires were finally extinguished a month later, nearly two hundred
thousand acres had burned and more than eleven hundred resi-
dences had been destroyed in San Diego County. Over half a million
people had been evacuated from their homes. It was an intense and
stressful time. The loss of life was tragic, as always. I was pleased,
however, that our efforts kept the situation from being even worse.
The incident also helped us understand and plan for how a terrorist
might use fire as a weapon in the future.

In addition, I was thrilled to have an opportunity to prove myself
and have it go so well. It was great to share that success with my dad.
I called him nearly every day on my commute home from work to tell
him about what I was working on. "I still can't believe," I said, "that I
went from being a firefighter to doing this."

Now sixty-three and retired from NCIS, my dad had mellowed
over the years. He enjoyed giving gifts to his grandkids and definitely
wanted a relationship with them. My brothers and I had even taught
him to say "I love you" at the end of our phone calls.

Dad and I were closer than we'd ever been. Yet so much of the
strong relationship I enjoyed with my dad was still based, at least in
my mind, on my accomplishments. I believed that because I was performing well at work, Dad could love and approve of me. It allowed
me to relax and relish our conversations. In the back of my mind,
however, was the sense that all of this was temporary, that I had to
keep raising the bar of my achievements or Dad would be disappointed in me and walk away again. That notion was a self-inflicted
barrier between us, more secure than any border crossing. I wasn't

willing to share my deeper feelings with Dad—or anyone—because I expected that sooner or later I'd get burned.

In truth, the same could be said about my relationship with God. My morning conversations with him on the fire escape and my increased dependence on him because of my job responsibilities had taken my faith to a new level. I looked forward to those prayer times and the encouragement the Lord gave me. I also felt that God had answered my prayers by allowing me to be more effective in our anti-terrorism work. Yet just as with my dad, I believed that a big part of the closeness I felt and the blessings I'd received was the result of my efforts. I was sure that if I slacked off even a little, God would soon be disappointed in me and disappear. The pressure to stay in Dad's and God's good graces was enormous.

It just meant that I had to work harder—so I did. It seemed that nearly every waking moment, I thought about where terrorists would strike next and how they would do it. Would it be a suicide bomber at a parade, the annual Rock 'n' Roll Marathon, or opening day for the Padres? Would a vehicle loaded with explosives crash into a federal building? Would the next attack involve chemical, nuclear, or radioactive weapons? It was my job to predict the next attack and then disrupt it. Fortunately, I was blessed with the chance to plug into San Diego's intelligence community. I started hearing details about terrorist activities abroad and on the East Coast, which helped me anticipate what might happen next in our area. I also joined an informal group made up of ten highly knowledgeable and dedicated officials from agencies across the security spectrum: the FBI, the NCIS, U.S. Customs and Border Protection, and the city's police department and sheriff's office. The more I coordinated with these people, the more I learned and the better prepared I was to prevent and respond to terrorist violence.

I knew I was making progress when I was asked to chair a working group charged with developing strategies to protect critical infrastructure: communications, transportation, energy, food and agriculture, emergency services, and more. We soon realized that one of our highest priorities was to better identify, monitor, and respond to potential threats at large-scale events. We needed cameras, license plate readers, vehicle barriers, boats, helicopters, and specially equipped vehicles. We had federal funds to purchase the equipment, but many of the agencies we worked with were private, so we couldn't just give them what they needed. Our solution was to buy the equipment ourselves, store it in a huge warehouse, and deploy it as appropriate, depending on the event. Keeping track of it all was a logistical headache, but it was a strategy that worked.

Although my work responsibilities weighed heavily on me, my position did allow me to experience occasional times of pure pleasure. One of those was the day I spent on a navy *Seawolf*-class nuclear submarine. I witnessed maneuvers from the bridge, peered through the periscope, inspected a nuclear reactor, and had lunch with the captain. I tried not to show it, but inside I was as excited as a kid on his birthday. Dad was happy for me—and a little bit jealous. "It doesn't get any better than that," he said.

In truth, so much of my life was going really well. I was gaining more and more confidence on the job each day and earning the respect of my colleagues. I knew I was making an important difference. I felt good about my relationships with both my earthly father and my heavenly one. However, I couldn't shake the nagging feeling that it would all fall apart one day. And I was troubled in another way. I was so dedicated to work that I had little time and energy for my family.

Despite my career success, was I blowing it as a husband and dad?

18

RISE UP AND WALK

So do not fear, for I am with you; do not be dismayed,
for I am your God.
—ISAIAH 41:10 NIV

5 P.M., TUESDAY, SEPTEMBER 22

KENAI PENINSULA

I'd finally admitted it—I was done. After toppling over the fallen tree and collapsing onto the ground, I had nothing left. But when I glanced up at Matt, narrowed eyes and tightly pressed lips told me he had no intention of giving up on his big brother. Instead, he would petition a higher authority.

Matt putt his right hand on my back, looked to the sky, and began to pray: "Lord, I know you have seen my struggles and my lack of belief at times, but I also know you've said you will never leave us or forsake us. I ask right now, in the name of Jesus Christ, that you give Greg the strength to make it out of here."

Matt removed his hand and spoke firmly into my ear. "Greg, you can do this," he said. "God will give you the strength."

To my surprise, my mind began to clear. Starting at my head and spreading across my chest and back and down to my legs and feet, I felt a surge of energy. In my mind I heard a voice, not one of despair or exhaustion, but of authority. "Rise up and walk," the voice said. "Your faith has healed you."

Okay, Lord, you win. I'll keep going. With Matt's help, I struggled to my feet and resumed the endless march.

I felt as if I were lifting hundred-pound weights with each step, but I resolved to look only straight ahead and not at my injuries. When I stretched out a hand to push a branch aside, however, I noticed fresh blood pouring from the cuff of my jacket and running down my fingers. I quickly turned away. Behind me, Matt continued to shout encouragement: "You can do this, Greg. I know you can."

The path we had chosen brought us uncomfortably close to a thick tree line that ran parallel with the slope of the mountains to the east. I tried to focus on the path in front of me, but my eyes kept shifting to the darkness just inside the trees. I imagined terrors lurking within. At every dark recess amid the canvas of greens and browns, my mind replayed horrific films of what I'd seen and felt after that monster charged me.

I was indescribably cold. Each gust that swept down the valley cut like knives through my blood-soaked jacket and pants. It felt as if someone were dumping a pitcher of ice water down my back. When I turned to look back at Matt, I saw that I was still leaving an obvious red trail. The cold and effects of trauma began playing more tricks on my psyche. I was convinced I could now taste and smell the iron-rich blood emanating from my clothing and being blown toward the trees hiding who knew what. I remembered the wolves we'd heard the night before. Whatever predator was downwind was receiving the unmistakable scent of fresh blood—a lot of it.

The USS *Indianapolis* was a cruiser that was torpedoed in the Pacific Ocean by a Japanese submarine in 1945, near the end of World War II. Approximately nine hundred survivors of the sinking plunged into shark-infested waters. Over the next four days, these men watched friends and shipmates suddenly disappear beneath the surface, one after the other, their presence replaced by a churning cauldron of red. Survivors said they were never more scared than when they waited for their turn to be lifted from waters full of circling sharks to the safety of the deck of a rescue amphibious aircraft. As I lurched toward what I hoped would be safety and survival, I understood the primal fear those men experienced. I fought my panicked state with a pair of mental mantras: *I can make it. I can make it.* Followed by: *The bear is not there. The bear is not there.*

Nothing had ever challenged me like this. It seemed as if I'd been walking for years across this inhospitable landscape. I raised my eyes to the top of the forest, and above it the mountain peaks. They climbed toward heaven like a staircase. It appeared I could step over the setting sun and the array of red and orange streaks it emitted and almost touch the face of God. How could I have just suffered such brutality and be surrounded by such beauty?

I was brought back to reality by more gentle encouragement from my brother: "You are doing good, Greg. You can do this."

The terrain ahead sloped slightly upward. Even this gradual rise was a massive, disheartening hurdle for my shattered body. I somehow mustered the strength to climb to the top of the knoll. When I crested the slope, I lifted my head, then fell to my knees.

Before me, just two hundred yards away, was the rocky shoreline of Skilak Lake. I heard from just around the bend of the bay the slap of waves against the sides of my brother's boat. Through God's mercy and a continuous stream of miracles, I had been granted the strength and will to walk out. We had overcome another impossible obstacle to my survival. I thanked the Lord that the grizzly had not attacked a second time during our slow and desperate escape.

It was a victory, but we were still a long way from being out of danger. I desperately needed help, and since we had no cell phone service here, help would be hard to come by.

I trudged on. Finally, twenty yards from the boat, my legs could no longer hold me. I fell headlong onto the rocky shore. Though I shook uncontrollably from the cold, for the first time since we'd embarked on the race for our lives out of the wilderness, I felt a sliver of peace. I rested my head on the hard ground and closed my eyes.

Matt was beside me in moments. "Are you all right?" he asked, his voice rising with worry. "We need to get you on the boat and get moving."

I lifted my head off the near-frozen rocks to survey the shoreline and, beyond it, the lake. Wind gusts continued to bend the trees along the edge of the forest. On Skilak Lake, those same gusts whipped foam and breaking wave crests into menacing whitecaps.

"Matt, with the wind chill and those whitecaps, I'll never survive a ten-mile boat ride. I'll die of hypothermia." I rolled onto my back. All of the bandages we'd applied at the scene of the attack were soaked through. "The first thing we need to do is get this bleeding stopped again. Then we need to get me warm." I asked Matt to retrieve the trauma kit and dry bag with all my extra clothing from the boat.

It seemed as if my entire body ached, but the worst, searing pain came from my right arm. I directed Matt to expose the wound. Four holes in my arm had been elongated by the grizzly's violent shaking. My lower arm looked as if it had been crushed in a vise. Everything was covered with fresh and dried blood. It was so grotesque that for a moment I had to turn away.

Naturally, because of my EMT background, I'd been responsible for preparing our medical supplies for the trip. In addition to all the usual items you'd find in a medical kit, I'd packed trauma dressings, sutures, compression bandages, medical tape, Kling and Kerlix bandage rolls, triangular bandages, penny-cutter scissors, gauze, and everything else required to stop bleeding from a significant injury. After the phone call from my dad and his urging to make sure I had everything I needed, I had doubled the number of trauma dressings—just in case. That foresight was about to pay off. Matt brought the medical trauma kit from the boat and grabbed the supplies I indicated. With me giving instructions, Matt dressed my arm perfectly within a minute. Silver dollar–sized bloodstains were soon oozing through the layers of dressing.

The idea of putting my right arm in a splint was almost too much to think about, but it had to be done. If we left it unsplinted, there was a real possibility that a piece of broken bone would come to rest against a main artery, cutting off the circulation. I could easily lose the arm. Despite excruciating pain, I repositioned my arm across my chest. I described to Matt how to make a sling and swath, which is placed around the neck and creates a kangaroo-style pouch to rest the arm in. When I lay back down on the cold, wet ground and released the weight of my arm into the sling, I could swear I heard angels sing. The reduction in pain was immediate. Matt had again done a great job.

Another small victory. Now, if we could only stop the bone-chilling cold that was rapidly spreading through my body. I shook as if I were suffering from a never-ending seizure. Images of climbers trapped in whiteout conditions on Everest danced through my mind.

I pointed to the dry bag. "Lay two of my jackets out on the ground so I can roll on top of 'em." Once I'd dragged myself onto the splayed jackets, Matt pulled more clothing from the dry bag and piled it on top of me, tucking everything in at my sides. Then he gently wrapped my head in a shroud.

Matt suddenly stiffened, his eyes on the lake. A second later, he jumped up and ran to the edge of the water. "Hey!" he yelled, waving his arms. "Help! Help!"

I hadn't heard or seen anything, but Matt obviously thought he'd spotted something. My brother continued to jump up and down and wave his rifle in a maniacal attempt to get the attention of whatever was out there.

After a minute of shouting with no results, Matt returned.

"Greg, I've got to go get help. The last thing I want to do is leave you here, but you're right, you probably wouldn't survive the trip. I think I saw some fishermen out there. I'm going to take the boat out. If I find them, maybe they'll have a satellite phone. If they don't, I'll go downriver to the place we had cell service and call 911."

I was barely able to speak through chattering teeth. "That," I said, "sounds like a lot of ifs." Matt didn't mention the biggest if, which was Mama Grizzly. The bear scat near the shore confirmed this area was no stranger to bears. If she was still stalking us, she could easily make her way to this beach. If she came after me, I doubted I'd have the strength to raise a rifle and defend myself.

I must have closed my eyes, because Matt was shaking me. "Greg, I'm going to leave you here with my rifle," he said, his voice stern, "but you have to roll onto your belly and stay awake to watch if the grizzly comes back."

I tried to process what my brother was saying. Finally the meaning of his words registered. I did not like this plan, not at all. I was to remain on the beach in a state of shock and hypothermia, soaked nearly head to toe in blood, and if necessary defend myself against a bloodthirsty, man-eating grizzly.

Yet we had no other options. It was literally do . . . or die.

BEN, CIARA, AND I LEFT Mari's house about nine o'clock that night. That was late for us on a school night, so I wanted to get home and get the kids to bed—especially Ciara, who was eight—right away.

Ciara put on the flannel Christmas pajamas that she wore year-round, and I tucked her into bed beneath her red-and-white comforter. Even though it was late, I wasn't going to skip our usual bedtime routine, which was to pray for Greg and Matt. I'd been praying for them with the kids at bedtime each night since Greg left. It was mainly for Greg and Matt's safety, but there was another reason I prayed. I wanted to alleviate any fears the kids might have, especially Ciara. Like me, Ciara was sensitive and intuitive about things. Though I'd tried to not let on about my own worries, over the last couple of weeks Ciara had also seemed uneasy about Greg's trip.

I knelt beside the bed and took Ciara's hands. We closed our eyes. "Father God," I said, "we just lift up Daddy and Uncle Matt and pray for your protection over them. We pray that you would keep them safe. We ask that you would protect them from other hunters' guns, that they would have fun, and that they would get their game."

It was Ciara's turn to pray. "Jesus," she said, "please bring Daddy home safe."

Ciara gave me a hug and kiss, then rolled onto her side and closed her eyes. I could tell our prayer had helped her feel a little more secure. To be honest, I felt better too. The uneasy feeling wasn't entirely gone, but I knew I'd done the only thing for Greg and Matt that I could. They were in God's good hands.

MATT TURNED AWAY FROM ME and walked toward the boat. I pulled my arm from the sling and wiped blood from my eyes so I could be ready to shoot. I rolled onto my belly and angled myself in the direction from which I believed the grizzly would appear. Next I crumpled one of the jackets into a ball, placed it on the rocks in front of me, and laid the stock of the rifle across it. This would be my line in the sand if the grizzly decided to return and finish me.

Suddenly, I heard a sound from across the water that I couldn't make out. Matt ran back up the beach toward me, waving his arms above his head and screaming, "Help! Help! Help!"

A few seconds later, the unrecognizable sound became recognizable: a boat motor. It was almost too good to be true. It appeared that once again God had intervened.

Soon a boat with three fishermen entered the shallows. One man, the boat's captain, jumped from the bow into two feet of water, grabbed the bowline, and splashed up the beach. After taking one look at my shredded carcass on the beach, he asked, "What the hell happened to him?"

Matt's answer was to the point: man sees bear, bear mauls man, man walks to boat half-dead. My brother quickly determined that none of the fishermen were doctors and that they had cell phones but no service. When the captain said he knew exactly the point on the river where he could acquire cell service, Matt said, "Sir, is there any way you could take your boat to that point and call 911 for us?"

The captain didn't hesitate: "Absolutely." Matt pulled out our GPS, told the captain our latitudinal and longitudinal coordinates, and handed him our topographic map. The captain and the other two fishermen hurried to hoist anchor and depart. Only minutes after they'd arrived, they were gone.

Matt returned to let me know what was happening. "Those fishermen are going to find cell service and call for help," he said. "So the good news is I don't have to leave you alone here." For that I was more than grateful. I let out a huge sigh of relief.

We figured the fishermen would be gone at least an hour. The task now was to keep me warm and awake until someone showed up. With layers of clothing stacked on me, the uncontrollable shaking had eased a bit, but I was still freezing. The pain, meanwhile, had become almost unbearable. It felt like someone had parked a car on my arm and that my fingertips were about to explode.

I had to face the possibility that something might still go wrong. The fishermen might not be able to find the right spot to make a call. Even if they did, emergency services might not be available. Plan B was carrying me to the boat and racing like hell for ten miles to the boat launch. Even if an ambulance was at the boat launch when we arrived, it would take at least another half hour to get me to an emergency room. The thought of waiting another two hours for medical attention with this pain and cold was intolerable.

I was comforted by the fact that people were working to save me. But what if their efforts were for nothing? With every minute that passed, my chances of survival dropped a little bit more. What if I did die out here? What if my next thoughts would be my last?

I pictured my wife and three children, their arms outstretched, beckoning me home. The thought that I might never see them again opened a chasm that cut to my core. Had I been a good father? A good husband? Who would take care of and protect my family? Had I told them often enough that I loved them? Had I told my dad I loved him that last time we spoke on the phone? Tears poured from my eyes. Instead of blood draining from my body, it now felt as if my soul was bleeding to death.

I had nowhere else to go with this pain. I prayed.

"God," I whispered, "I know you are here and have always been here for me. You showed me when I was a child that you were real, and I know you've stood by my side even to this very moment. But this is my truth right now, Lord. I have been pounded to the bottom of the sea by a tidal wave of fear. Daddy, your little boy is scared."

19

A GOOD FATHER

A good father is one of the most unsung, unpraised, unnoticed,
and yet one of the most valuable assets in our society.
—BILLY GRAHAM

During the summer of 2009, my dad was talking with one of his buddies from his NCIS days. This friend now worked on the admiral's staff at Navy Region Southwest, which was headquartered on the San Diego waterfront and responsible for naval installations in California and five other western states. Dad mentioned my antiterrorism work with the city. He probably bragged a little.

The friend leaned forward. "Have Greg give me a call," he said. "I might have an opening for him."

I did, and he did. The admiral and his staff were looking for an antiterrorism officer.

Among other things, Navy Region Southwest was charged with protecting the largest naval fleet concentration on the West Coast. Nowhere would you find more ships, aircraft carriers, submarines, aircraft, and special operations personnel in one place. I knew with the military's ramped-up efforts in Afghanistan and Iraq that the navy would be a prime target. If I became their antiterrorism officer, it would mean joint operations with NCIS and the FBI Joint Terrorism Task Force in San Diego, a significant threat environment, and the responsibility to stay one step ahead of a cunning and sophisticated enemy.

When I was offered the position, the answer was easy: "I'll absolutely take the job."

A huge part of the appeal was the chance to have an even greater impact in the world of antiterrorism. It would fulfill the vision I'd had eight years before at the World Trade Center in New York when I promised to dedicate my life to protecting U.S. citizens. I also loved the idea of in some ways continuing my dad's work. At NCIS, he had been part of the post-investigation security teams after the Khobar Towers terrorist bombing in Saudi Arabia in 1996, which killed nineteen U.S. Air Force personnel, and the bombing of the navy destroyer USS *Cole* in a Yemen harbor in 2000, which killed seventeen American sailors. In a sense, I was following in Dad's footsteps.

Starting in September of that year, I was tasked with defending the navy's West Coast fleet from terrorists. I also led the navy's Command Threat Working Group, which coordinated with local, state, and federal security and law enforcement agencies to protect the navy and citizens of greater San Diego. The pressure to succeed had suddenly skyrocketed.

Special events were among my key assignments. One of the most significant occurred less than two years after I came on board. Soon after a team of Navy SEALs took out the world's most wanted man, Osama bin Laden, in Pakistan on May 2, 2011, I learned that naval special operations command and the carrier group that supported them planned to commemorate the achievement—at the USS *Midway* Museum, the retired aircraft carrier that was docked at the Navy

Pier in San Diego, within view of our office. I couldn't imagine a group of men and women that al-Qaeda terrorists would be more motivated to attack. I had ten days to prepare.

We deployed our usual assets and then some, which included snipers atop adjoining buildings and on the *Midway*, naval security Fleet Anti-Terrorism Security Team (FAST) boats on the water, divers, Customs and Border Protection agents on both land and in the water, military helicopters in the sky, NCIS and FBI agents mixing in the crowd near the *Midway* gangplank, and K-9 dogs in the parking lot sweeping for explosives in cars. We also had tactical teams standing by, ready to deploy if there was a terrorist strike. I was in the command post at our headquarters across the street, helping coordinate everyone's movements and praying hard.

Thankfully, the event came off without a hitch. I was relieved that some of our nation's finest military representatives could enjoy a well-deserved celebration, one unblemished by tragedy.

That fall, senior navy and Marine Corps leadership, along with congressional leaders and first responder senior staff from across Southern California, assembled on the *Midway* to mark the tenth anniversary of 9/11. I was also responsible for security at the annual Navy Bay Bridge Run/Walk. Each May, Navy Region Southwest hosted the four-mile trek across the Coronado Bridge to raise funds for quality-of-life programs for military personnel and their families. My final year of handling security for this event was stressful. It was the one-year anniversary of the Boston Marathon bombing. We had ten thousand navy and Marine Corps men and women and their families running in a concentrated area, a significant vulnerability. We avoided disaster at these events as well.

If that wasn't enough to keep me busy, I worked with an FBI intelligence analyst and a special operations official in Washington, D.C., to establish an intelligence information-sharing network. It changed how San Diego distributed and processed information about terrorist threats, techniques, and tactics. The network wasn't part of my regular job duties but something I did on my own. I thought it would help all of us do a better job. I tried to take a servant's mind-set to my work. My dad once told me, "If you're willing to come up with the idea, do all of the work, and then give someone else the credit, you can accomplish anything." For me, the bottom line was doing whatever it took to protect our people from the bad guys.

Some of my coworkers thought I took my job too seriously. One joked, "You should be encased in glass with instructions that say, 'Break only in case of a real terrorist threat.'" But few of the people I worked with had been on the scene of a terrorist attack. They hadn't seen the Twin Towers reduced to a twisted pile of steel that served as a mass grave for three thousand fathers, mothers, daughters, and sons. They didn't truly understand what we were up against and what could happen if our efforts fell short.

I didn't expect them to understand my passion. To be honest, I didn't expect anyone to understand it, not even my wife. Rhea had always been supportive of me and my obsession with antiterrorism work. She hadn't complained about the move to San Diego or the long work hours or my lack of energy at home. She easily could have, because I'd never fully explained how this was something I had to do, how the images of 9/11 still burned in my soul. I hadn't told her because I was holding back part of myself, just as I'd held back with Dad and with God. I'd been hurt so deeply when my dad left that I couldn't risk being hurt that way again. I lost my anchor that day. I decided that if I couldn't trust family, I couldn't trust anyone but myself.

I also hadn't let Rhea see how deeply I feared failing as a father. I realized that I was doing the same thing with my kids that I was doing with everyone else I cared about—trying to have a loving relationship yet keeping a distance so that if something happened to pull us apart, I would survive the wound. I knew there was something wrong with this picture but didn't know what to do about it. Were my kids destined to grow up feeling the way I did, like a loner who was unworthy of love?

Our stucco, ranch-style home was built into the side of a San Diego hill overlooking a verdant valley. It offered an amazing view of avocado and eucalyptus trees, as well as nearby Mount Helix. Increasingly, however, I found myself missing out on the scenery. I was getting home later and later and feeling more and more exhausted. One day, after I drove up our driveway and backed my Toyota FJ60 Land Cruiser into the space next to the basketball hoop, I put my arms and head on the steering wheel and closed my eyes. I knew my family was waiting for me, but I had nothing to give them.

What is going on with me? I wondered. *I think I'm doing what I'm supposed to do, ensuring my country's security. But I'm so busy and overwhelmed that I'm missing out on my kids' lives. I'm missing their practices, their school events. In my pursuit of what I believe is my calling, have I become what I feared most?*

The idea that I might be destroying my family was more than I could bear. I felt that to choose one, either country or family, would be to fail the other. The pressure was too much. Had my dad faced these same decisions with his job when he decided to leave us? Had my dad also concluded that his family might be better off without him?

I began to weep.

* * *

RHEA, THE KIDS, AND I attended the nondenominational Foothills Christian Church in El Cajon. We always sat near the front and enjoyed the worship music, teaching, and informal atmosphere. I also got involved in a weekly men's Bible study. I figured I needed all the spiritual help I could get.

The Bible study is where I met Tim, a soft-spoken husband and father who ran an upholstery business. The more we talked, the more comfortable I became around him. He and I started showing up early at the study to drink coffee, chat, and share a few of our concerns and struggles. I learned we had similar deep father wounds.

In June 2012, Rhea and I were making our way toward the sanctuary exit doors at the end of a Sunday morning service when Tim approached. He gave us both a quick hug, then pulled me aside.

"Greg, I've been meaning to tell you something," he said, his expression serious. "The Lord's been putting it on my heart." He paused to look me directly in the eyes. "This is what he wants me to say: 'Greg, I think you're a good father.'"

I was taken aback. I had no reason to doubt Tim's sincerity. I knew he was a man of strong faith. Was God really speaking to me? It was the first time anyone had given me a message from the Lord since I'd spoken to the pastor with Janelle's mom.

A tear slid down my cheek. I had to get out of there before I started bawling. When I told Rhea about Tim's words, she said, "I've always thought you were the best dad I've ever known."

After that day, I started making time to visit Tim at his house. As he pulled fabric over furniture, I talked. I shared more about my dad leaving, the divorce, and how it affected me. It was a relief to finally allow another person to see a sliver of the pain I carried inside.

I wanted to believe what God had said through Tim and what Rhea had echoed. I was moved to receive such a message. Yet I wasn't ready to accept it. I was sure I could accomplish almost anything, but the concept of me being a good father still seemed beyond my reach. I desperately wanted to be that kind of dad for my kids, but in my heart—despite what the people around me were saying—I was certain that I would somehow fail and bring pain to my children.

The threat of that potential failure weighed heavily on me. I realized that the time and energy I was devoting to my job was only increasing. I believed wholeheartedly in my antiterrorism work, but what was the cost? After much agonized thinking and prayer, I finally made a necessary decision—I talked to Rhea about finding a position in security with a slower tempo. As usual, she supported me 100 percent.

About a year and a half later, the Matthews family was on the move again, this time to Plano, Texas. I had accepted a job as antiterrorism officer for the Southwest Division of the U.S. Army Corps of Engineers. I would be responsible for protecting dams, hydropower generation plants, locks, and intercoastal waterways in Texas, Oklahoma, New Mexico, Arkansas, Louisiana, and parts of Missouri. I would still play a vital role in a region of our nation's security, but the work would be a little less overwhelming and allow me to devote more of myself to my family.

Did I believe deep down that I was a good father? The answer was still no. But I was trying, both to believe it and to be it.

RESCUE

When he calls to me, I will answer him; I will be with him in
trouble; I will rescue him and honor him.
—PSALM 91:15 ESV

7:15 P.M., TUESDAY, SEPTEMBER 22
SKILAK LAKE

Yes, I was afraid. As I lay on the beach, my body shutting down, confronting the reality that I could be minutes away from dying, I was terrified—in part for myself, but so much more over what my death would mean for each member of my family. Yet, when I prayed to God—"Daddy, your little boy is scared"—the fear began to fade. I felt the Lord's assurance that no matter what happened, he would be with me and the people I loved. The rising panic was replaced by a welcome blanket of calm.

Once again, my desperate words had been heard. I resolved that as long as I was alive, I would fight to keep it that way.

During my career as a firefighter, I had learned that in an emergency there is always something more you can do to affect the outcome. I was near the end of my ability to do anything physically, but I could still use my brain. What was the next step? I tried to block out the pain and concentrate. Then it hit me. Shadows were stretching across the lake; sunset was less than an hour away. If a boat or helicopter *was* headed our way, our rescuers would need a way to see us. I talked with Matt. We decided we needed a signal fire.

My brother dragged driftwood to the lake edge, about thirty-five yards from me. Then he grabbed his hatchet and handsaw and moved up the bank into the brush to cut young pine limbs and green marsh brush. It was satisfying to at least take another positive step.

Matt was stacking the fire fuel when the distant hum of a boat motor reached our ears. It was the sweetest sound I'd heard all day. The fishermen were back. But had they been able to get through to anyone?

The captain killed his motor and glided the boat toward shore. Another man yelled from the bow: "We called 911! They're dispatching a fire department boat and an EMS rescue helicopter!"

If I'd been able to stand, I would have run to those three men and given them the biggest hugs they'd ever received. Instead, as I lay on the beach, tears of joy streamed down my face. I pulled off the jacket covering my head and in a voice barely louder than a whisper said, "Thank you! And thank you, God!"

Could it be true? Could this whole nightmare really be coming to an end? I was afraid to even think it.

Four pairs of hands made quick work of gathering the remaining fuel for the fire, and before long they had a seven-foot pile of limbs on the beach. Though blood continued to run down my face and neck and I was still shaking uncontrollably, I didn't feel nearly as cold as before. I lay in silence, listening intently for the familiar *whop, whop, whop* of rotor blades.

Matt and the fishermen determined that when the helicopter approached, the pilot would likely attempt to land right on the beach. Matt knew from his air force experience that it wouldn't take an object of any great size to strike a tail rotor blade, which could quickly unbalance its rotation and lead to disaster. My brother picked out a landing site and organized the others. They cleared small rocks, debris, and driftwood from the shore and marked the area with a giant X. Despite my condition, I smiled with pride as I watched Matt work and direct his team. He'd never stopped thinking about what else he could do to help me win this battle for my life. I loved him for that and more.

To conserve heat and try to quit shaking, I curled into a fetal position beneath the pile of clothing. I imagined the faces of the helicopter pilot and medical crew, men and women who were putting themselves at risk to help me. I couldn't supervise the landing zone or carry their gear. I couldn't prevent Matt or the fishermen from accidentally walking into an invisible, spinning tail rotor blade. I felt I was letting everyone down by not doing my part to ensure they would make it back to their families safely.

This line of thinking wasn't doing anybody any good. I forced myself to forget about what I couldn't do and focus on what I could do. I prayed.

In the distance, a sound like the low roar of thunder echoed against the valley walls. I yanked a jacket off my head and strained to decipher the noise. It did sound like thunder, but had a rhythmic thump imbedded within its low growl. A huge smile broke out over my face when I realized the thumps were not thunder but the sound of rotor blades slicing through the sky. The truth was confirmed when from down the beach I heard the *woof* of the fire being lit, along with excited shouts from my brother and the others. I tried to raise my head to spot the helicopter, but the angled slope of the beach blocked my view. All I could do was listen and pray that the pilot would see our signal fire. I felt as if all of us were holding our breath and trying to will the helicopter into view.

At last, the shout I'd been waiting for erupted from down the beach: "There it is!"

Another wise choice that Matt and I made in our preparations for this trip was to include a flare gun among our supplies. Matt had it in his hand now and raised it to the sky. While on my back, I watched a glowing red tail climb high above us, then arc gracefully over the lake. Seconds later, a second ball of red-hot phosphorus soared into the Alaska sky.

The whine of a turbine engine drifted over the tops of the trees toward us. Matt and the fishermen waved their arms and jumped up and down, trying to catch the pilot's attention. "God," I prayed, "please let the pilot see us."

Suddenly, not more than five hundred feet off the ground, an A-Star helicopter thundered right over me. It was an incredible sight. Cheers and whoops of excitement sounded from the beach as the pilot jetted across the water, then rolled the helicopter into a steep right turn and returned to our position. The pilot gradually reduced altitude and did a flyover to confirm we were his target and to inspect the landing area. He made an additional high-recon flyover before moving into a final approach to land. The helicopter entered a slow, descending 180-degree left turn until its nose was in line with the landing site. When the aircraft was seventy-five feet above the water, the high-pitched whir of the turbine engine and the whine of the rotors were earsplitting. At that moment I didn't care if they made me deaf for the rest of my life.

Slowly, the helicopter eased down until its skids gently touched the smooth rocks on the shore. The pilot did a pedal turn to dig the skids in and level the landing surface. Sand and water pelted my face, but I didn't mind a bit. Both helicopter doors slid open. Before I knew it, a nurse and a paramedic, both in flight suits, were kneeling by my side. The paramedic peeled back the layers of clothes and examined the bandages on my neck, head, arm, and leg, as well as the splint. "You guys didn't leave anything for me to do," she said. "Who stopped the bleeding and treated all your wounds?"

I mumbled that my brother and I had worked together.

"Well, you guys did a great job," she said. "Now all we have to worry about is getting an IV started to get you some pain meds and fluids."

After four unsuccessful attempts to find a vein—three in my left arm and one in my foot—I was ready to stand up and walk to the helicopter by myself. I didn't blame the nurse, who kept jabbing me with a needle. I'd lost so much blood that my blood vessels had constricted. Locating a vein was nearly impossible. I also knew that protocol dictated we couldn't get into the warm helicopter until IV access was established. Yet I had reached my limit.

"If this next one doesn't work," I said, "don't even think about looking at my neck or chest because it ends here. I can live with the pain and I know my blood pressure is stable enough to keep me from going further into shock. We are getting on that helicopter, IV or no IV."

Just then, I looked to my right and saw a new face. He had a big smile, which I could just make out through his bushy beard. His eyes were kind. I asked, "Who are you, sir?"

He grabbed my hand. "Randy. I live around here."

"You live around here, in the middle of the woods." It was a statement, not a question. Who was this guy, Grizzly Adams?

"I live close enough to have heard the report of your attack over the radio. I beat feet over here to see if I could lend a hand." His smile grew even bigger and brought a sense of calm to the chaos I felt. Out of the blue, a Bible verse came to me: "For you know not when you entertain angels." As far as I was concerned, God had just sent a guardian angel to attend me.

Still holding my hand, Randy reassured me that this was an excellent crew and they would take good care of me. "How do you know," I asked, "if this is a good crew or not?"

"I work in the emergency department of the hospital you'll be flown to."

Warm tears began to slide down my face. "I don't know where you came from, Randy, but thank you for being here for me."

Randy had distracted me from the efforts of the nurse. On his sixth try, and third in my foot, the needle had found a vein. Pain medication was at last flowing into my body.

The paramedic and my brother peeled away the clothing piled on top of me and rolled me into a soft stretcher. The instant that warm layer of clothing was removed, I felt as if I'd been thrown into a deep freeze. Matt knelt beside me, took my hand, and gave my wounds a last visual inspection. He looked at me and tried to speak, but no words came out.

I squeezed his hand. "It's okay, Matt, say it."

"I've got to leave," he finally said, "and let these folks take care of you." I could tell my brother was fighting to keep his emotions in check. "We're almost there, Greg. You just hang on."

Tears traced with blood slid down my cheek. Pulling my brother close, I whispered, "Thank you, Matt, for saving my life."

Matt gave me a wink, released my hand, and grabbed a handle on the litter. He and the crew carried me to the waiting helicopter and slid me in.

In moments, we were airborne. The top of the helicopter had a clear plexiglass window that revealed a dusky sky above rapidly spinning blades. "Relax and enjoy the ride," the nurse said. "We'll be there in twenty minutes."

The pain soon subsided and my body at last began to warm up. I took the pain-free opportunity to lift my head and examine my rescue chariot. I couldn't quite see out the windscreen, but the instrumentation and forward-looking radarscope were visible. If I was pushed any farther down the gurney, my feet would be resting on the pilot's lap. No doubt because of the drugs kicking in, this seemed like the funniest thing in the world.

Fifteen minutes into our flight, the medic and nurse started preparing me for the landing. The paramedic got on the radio and gave a report on my condition to the emergency room staff: "Central Peninsula, this is Air One. We have a forty-eight-year-old male who has been attacked by a grizzly bear. Patient's chief complaint is lacerations and bite marks to the head, face, neck, and extremities. Bleeding has been controlled and vital signs are stable. Currently we have the patient on a non-rebreather flowing ten liters and have established an IV with a total of fifteen milligrams of morphine on board. ETA is approximately five minutes."

Once a pilot, always a pilot—on our approach, I pretended that I was flying myself to the hospital. I could tell that our pilot was good. I barely felt his inputs to flight controls. Moments later, we were on the ground.

The wide-open spaces of Alaska gave way to a feeling of claustrophobia as I was hauled off the helicopter and surrounded by those tasked with saving me. The air filled with the buzz of medical jargon. I'm sure there were a few horrified grimaces from those looking down at me, but I didn't care. I was safe in the hands of professionals.

The nurse and paramedic helped roll the gurney into the emergency room. Supervisors called out orders for X-rays, CAT scans, and bloodwork. Two men dressed in surgical garb introduced themselves as Matt and Anderson.

I could have predicted the first question: "Who looks worse, you or the bear?"

"My brother and I put up a good fight," I said.

Surprised that the bloody mess lying on the gurney could actually talk, my two new friends struck up a conversation. Both were avid Alaska hunters and fishermen. Within ten minutes, I had an invitation to come back to Alaska and do a little fishing for "reds," their salmon of choice. Matt and Anderson put me at ease until I was rolled down the hall to the X-ray room.

The doctors were concerned about the possibility that the grizzly's fangs had penetrated my skull and injured my brain. I'm sure my closest friends would have told the doctors that any brain damage they discovered had been there long before the bear went to work on me. Nevertheless, they X-rayed my arm, leg, and head. Afterward, they sent me into the CAT scan tunnel. Back in the emergency room, a nurse grabbed my hand and told me how lucky I was to be in the hospital that day.

"What is so lucky about all of this for me?" I asked.

"It just so happens that the surgeon on call tonight is one of the best head and neck surgeons around. He's also double board certified as an accomplished plastic surgeon. He is known for his ability to operate on people who have experienced significant trauma to their neck, face, and head. That's why you're lucky. I'm part of his team and we're going to take super-good care of you, Greg."

It seemed that the Lord was still orchestrating events in my favor.

A distinguished-looking gentleman poked his head over the nurse's shoulder. "Greg, I'm your surgeon. I'll be taking care of you in the operating room." He grabbed my hand and looked me straight in the eyes. "I have done this type of surgery hundreds of times and I am going to make you good as new. I've got to scrub up now and get everything ready. You just try and relax and before you know it you'll be out of surgery. Do you have any questions for me?"

"No, sir, I just want to say thank you for taking care of me." He squeezed my hand, winked, and walked away.

Matt was here now, but I wished Rhea and the kids could be by my side. They knew nothing about what was happening. I was saddened to think I would not be in their prayers during the surgery.

I imagined a stranger calling Rhea and telling her I'd been attacked by a grizzly bear. I realized I could not let that happen. Rhea needed to hear my voice. I had to be the one to explain about the attack and let her know I would be okay.

With my left hand, I grabbed Matt by the arm. "I need my cell phone," I said. "I have to call Rhea right now and let her know I'm all right."

"Greg, you're about to go into surgery. Give me the number and I'll call her after you get prepped."

"No, that isn't going to happen. I need to call my wife right now or I'm not going into the operating room."

Matt knew better than to argue with his older brother when he'd made up his mind. "Where's your phone?"

"Unfortunately, it's in the bag of expensive hunting clothing they cut off me when they were treating me on the beach." Matt started rummaging through the personal effects that had ridden with me in the helicopter. The staff began to wheel me through the double doors of the hallway leading to the operating room.

"Matt," I cried out, "I need to make that call!" Matt ran up, shoved his arm between the two nurses at my side, and handed me my phone. The gurney was still moving. I pressed the power button, closed my eyes, and prayed that the Lord would power the phone up one more time. It was late back in Texas and I knew Rhea would be in bed. The phone rang three times before she answered in a sleepy voice.

"Babe," I said, "it's me."

"Hi," Rhea said, her voice still groggy but getting clearer. "How is everything going?"

"Babe, I'm going to be okay." (Nothing good comes from a conversation that starts with those words.) "There was an accident. I'm at the hospital getting ready to go into surgery. I'm going to be okay."

For a moment, all was silent.

"WHAT?" Rhea shouted. "What happened to you?"

"Um, babe, I was attacked by a grizzly bear. But I am going to be just fine."

"Oh my goodness!" My wife began to sob. I had trouble understanding what she was trying to say.

"Babe, I just had to call you so you could hear my voice before I go into surgery. I promise you that I'm going to be okay and that I'm going to come home to you." I fought against the urge to cry myself. "Babe, listen, they are rolling me into surgery right now so I have to go. I love you, sweetheart, and I will call you as soon as I'm out of surgery. Call Matt and he can give you all the details. I love you, baby. Tell the kids I love them very much, okay?"

Rhea was still crying. It broke my heart to put her through that. Her last words were, "I love you, babe. I'm praying right now." Tears streamed down my face as I handed the phone back to Matt. The end of the gurney met cold, stainless steel doors, then pushed through as I was wheeled into the operating room.

21

I WAS THERE

For as the heavens are higher than the earth,
so are my ways higher than your ways and my thoughts
than your thoughts.
—ISAIAH 55:9 ESV

A huge, dark monster dragged my body through a river of blood. Black killer's eyes stared into mine. Impossibly long white fangs thrust at my throat. Was this a nightmare or was it real?

It dawned on me—as I gulped air and the all-too-real images danced crazily in my mind like a horror-movie highlight reel—that I was sitting up in a bed. I blinked and tried to fight off the panic. My eyes darted back and forth, taking in indistinguishable dark shapes that surrounded me. Where was I?

I was in a room. As my eyes adjusted to the darkness, the vague shapes began to snap into focus. A large black-and-white minute-hand clock, almost identical to the ones I grew up with in school classrooms, hung on the wall directly in front of me. The time was 1:40. Below that, a series of white cabinets extended across the wall.

A flat-screen TV was mounted to their right. Farther to the right was the outline of an open door, and behind that, a sink.

But what was to the right of that? Just a few feet away, a dark, horizontal something or someone was against the wall—I couldn't make it out. Instantly, the terrible images I'd just endured flooded my mind once again. Sweat and the shakes returned with a vengeance. What was in here with me?

Frantic, I looked for a way to escape. On the left, next to my bed, was a metal tray. My cell phone rested on the tray. I grabbed it with my left hand and pressed the "home" button. The screen came to life. The light revealed even more details about the room—but I would not look at the unknown something to my right. The phone in my hand trembled. I quickly set the phone back down. The light blinked off, again plunging me into darkness.

What was over there?

Hesitantly, I picked up my phone a second time. My index finger touched the home button. I traced my finger along the outline of the button, but I couldn't muster the courage to press it. I extended the phone in the direction of the dark mass and tried to will the power on. I imagined new horrors that the light would illuminate.

I had to know. I pressed the button.

It was my brother. He lay on a rollaway bed against the wall, still in his clothes, sound asleep. I shifted the phone to get a better view. Matt's clothes were covered with dried blood. I was reminded of the many blood-saturated bodies I'd seen as an EMT. The difference was that the blood I was looking at this time was mine.

Suddenly it all came back to me—the hunt, the charging grizzly, trying to defend myself against a vicious attacker, the bleeding and pain, and, at last, my rescue. Now I was in a hospital intensive care unit. To see the room better, I held up the phone with my right hand.

Excruciating pain immediately shot through my arm. I transferred the phone back to my left hand and examined my arm. I was shocked at what I saw. My forearm was wrapped in bandages soaked with blood where the grizzly's massive fangs had sunk all the way through. Tears fell from my eyes at the awful memory.

I dropped the phone onto my lap and with my left hand probed my face, neck, and head. My face and neck were completely covered in bandages. The last spot I explored was under my chin and across my neck. My fingers felt moist, no doubt from the tears running down my face. I had no idea of the extent of my wounds and injuries but I knew it wasn't good.

It must have been only a short time since they'd rolled me out of surgery. I knew I was still feeling the effects of the anesthesia because I could hold my head up for only a few seconds before it fell limp back to the pillow. Every minute or so I heard the cycling of a pump next to the bed. I guessed that it contained morphine.

I put my phone on flashlight mode and was shocked at the sight of my left hand—the fingers I'd used to examine my neck were dripping blood. My cell phone crashed to the floor. How bad were my injuries? Was I going to recover? Were the doctors just waiting for me to die?

I was afraid if I moved I'd tear something open, so I kept my body still and buried my face in my pillow. All I wanted was my wife and kids by my side. I had no idea if I would ever see my family again or how badly the grizzly had disfigured my face. During the attack, I had felt flesh being ripped from my head and face, but to what extent I could only imagine. Would I go through life with people staring at me like I was some monster? Would my family look upon me with pity? Grief washed over me. I pictured horrific scars that I would wear for the rest of my life—if I survived.

The one thing I was certain of was that I'd been torn apart by a grizzly. As to whether I would live or die, only the doctors knew. I began to sob. I feared that my only way out of this hospital was through the morgue. Like a young child awakened from a nightmare, unable to separate truth from imagination, I sat in the dark and hoped that if I blinked enough times it would all go away. It didn't. My nightmare was my truth.

Lord, I prayed, *did you put me through all of that trauma and pain only to watch me die?* I'd felt alone for most of my life, but now the sense of abandonment overwhelmed me.

God, where are you?

I MUST HAVE DOZED. I woke up, still in the hospital bed, still in the dark, my brother still asleep against the wall. As my eyes adjusted to the dim light, I suddenly realized that there was another figure with me, a person sitting close on my bed.

It was Dad.

He wrapped his arms around me and pressed his face so tight against my neck that I could feel his whiskers. It was the desperate embrace of a man who'd feared he'd never see his son again. Dad wore a white shirt and sat with his feet on the floor, his body half turned toward me. As he held me he began to gently shake. I realized he was crying.

It had all happened so fast. I hadn't had time to think about how Dad got here so quickly. But I was both thrilled that he had come and taken aback by his tears.

"Dad," I said, "what's wrong?"

"I almost lost you today," he whispered, his face still hidden in my neck. "I feel part of that is my fault. I've tried my entire life to be there for you, to protect you from every danger, but I couldn't be there today for you. I'm so sorry I wasn't there to face that bear with you."

He sniffed and continued. "There are certain moments, beyond all other moments, where a dad *has* to be there for his child. And if the father isn't there to come between that danger and his child, the father fails, and the pain and hurt fall on the one he deeply loves."

Now Dad was openly sobbing. "I'm sorry I wasn't there, Greg. I'm sorry, I'm sorry, I'm sorry."

I had never seen my dad cry like this—or heard such an unequivocal expression of love. I squeezed him tight. Tears poured from my eyes. This was a moment I'd longed for ever since that day Dad had driven out of our driveway. We held each other for several seconds before I slowly released my embrace, eased him back, and looked into his eyes.

"Dad, you *were* there for me. Everything you did to raise me and teach me as a young boy was what I drew on to survive that attack. You taught me everything I know about the outdoors. Those summer camping trips you took us on taught me about being in the woods and how to survive. You demonstrated how to remain calm, think through stressful decisions, and come up with solutions. You taught me to never give up fighting for what I believe in. I applied those lessons today, Dad. Because of what you showed me, I'm alive.

"The biggest reason I know you were there is that you were the one who taught me that I could do anything if I set my mind to it." I pulled my father close again and pressed my lips to his ear. "Dad, I love you, and I want to thank you for being there to save my life today. You were there, Dad. I promise, you were there."

As I held my dad and peeked over his shoulder, I saw that blood from my bandaged arm had soaked into the back of his shirt. I pulled away again. I wanted to say that I was sorry for ruining his shirt.

I never got those words out. You see, Dad wasn't Dad anymore. Instead, I was looking into the face of Jesus.

He was clean-shaven, with shoulder-length dark hair. He wore a white robe. The room was too dark for me to fully make out his features, except for the eyes—blue and penetrating.

There was nothing in his appearance, however, that told me who he was. Somehow, I just knew.

You might think that finding the Lord suddenly sitting close to you would inspire a sense of honor and awe, or maybe reverent fear. I'm sorry to say that isn't where my muddled mind went. Part of me felt shame. I couldn't look into those eyes for longer than a moment. I had to turn away.

Most of me, though, was angry.

Why, I thought, *are you showing up now? Where were you when that six-hundred-pound beast was ripping me apart? Why didn't you keep the bear from charging or send it in another direction or at least intercede and stop the mauling? Where were you when I was screaming in pain and the grizzly was carving me up with her fangs? And why are you interrupting one of the most important moments of my life with my dad?*

Rage blew through me like an arctic gust. This was not the father in heaven I had grown to love, or the creator I had pinned my hopes on and learned to depend on. I felt like an ant on an anthill, with God holding a magnifying glass over me. Had he kept me alive just so he could look me in the eyes as he abandoned me forever?

Without a word, Jesus pulled me into an embrace. I heard and felt him crying, just like my dad.

None of this made sense. I tried to pull away. The Lord's arms around me held fast. I struggled harder to break his hold, without success. My anger returned and boiled over. *You abandoned me*, I thought. *Just like when my dad drove away, you let this happen. I have no desire to be near you.*

I was fighting to escape. I'd reached a verdict in my mind and declared God guilty. I wanted nothing to do with him. And still he would not let go.

I'm not sure if this strange wrestling match continued for minutes or just seconds. All I know is that I reached a point of exhaustion. An unexpected thought entered my mind: *If I'm about to die and if I'm going to heaven, maybe I should just accept it.*

Finally, I had no strength left to fight with. I relaxed and fell into Jesus's arms crying, my head on his shoulder. "Where were you, Lord?" I asked, my voice hollow. "I called for you but you never came. Couldn't you see what was happening to me? Were my cries not desperate enough for you to come running like you always promised? Couldn't you hear or recognize one of your own son's voices desperately calling out for help from his daddy in heaven? Yet you never showed. You did the same thing when I was a little boy."

I lifted my head and found the courage to again look at Jesus. His eyes welled with tears, but that didn't stop the runaway freight train in my mind. My emotions erupted like a geyser. "You promised you would never leave or forsake me," I shouted, "that you would always be there to protect me. You lied, Lord. You lied!"

I tried to catch my breath through my tears. Jesus began to sob.

"Why," I asked, "are you crying, Lord?"

His voice was calm and soft, yet it captured my attention like nothing I'd heard before. "Greg," he said, "I am crying because of the emotional and physical pain you have gone through, but even more because you are convinced that I abandoned you at the moment you needed me most."

As crazy as it sounds, I began to argue with Jesus. "Look at my face," I said. "Look at my head, my neck, my arm, my leg, and tell me you were there."

"Greg, I never left your side for a second during the entire attack. I was protecting you when you didn't even know I was protecting you. I felt every bite and every claw that ripped into you. I experienced every feeling running through your mind and heart and I felt the fear and terror surging through your veins. I was there to hold you close during your desperate screams for help. I became your shield."

I shook my head. "I don't understand. If what you say is true, why do I look like this? Why did you let the attack happen?"

"Sometimes things happen in this world you will not understand. Some things bring great pain, but I can assure you that, in the end, what has happened here will bring you far greater joy than pain."

I simply stared. "Lord, I am so confused. If you were there, where is the evidence?"

Jesus still cradled me in his arms. Tears slid down his cheeks. "My son, upon seeing the grizzly, you chose not to hide but to face the bear. Why? You chose to face the bear because you knew the bear could charge down the trail to your brother, who was unaware of the danger. You chose love and courage instead of self. I was the one to place those things in your heart, just when it needed to be done. Your brother is alive and unharmed. You had no idea if those bears would reach your brother, but you chose to not let that happen. I was there.

"Without much time to process, you made the decision on which weapon to choose from the three you had available to face the bear. You chose your rifle and trusted in the bullet you reloaded with your own hands. I gave you those hands to produce that bullet that would save your life. The very fingers that measured the powder, that placed the primer and seated the two-hundred-grain bullet, were the same hands I made in your mother's womb. I was there also, Greg.

"When that bear charged in a blur and there was no time but to raise the rifle and fire that one single round, I was there. When that single bullet traveled into the mouth of the bear where I directed it, dislodging her lower left fang and shattering her lower jawbone, I was there. My son, that bear did not have full use of her jaw when she reached you. That was my plan and purpose in having you choose the rifle and then directing your shot. When you went blind and could not see or even hear anything during the most terrifying points of the attack, you were in my arms like you are now. I shielded you. I protected your heart and mind and the future of your family by not allowing you to witness and hear the most terrible parts of that attack. I was looking out for you even then, Greg.

"While I held you on the ground, in the midst of the bear's fury, I sent your brother with the perfect measure of courage and love that I placed in his heart for you. I have always said there is no greater love than a brother who willingly lays down his life. I was there, Greg. I sent him. When you thought you were dying and all hope was lost, I gave you the strength and composure to walk your brother through stopping your bleeding and providing the medical attention you needed. As you lay in a pool of blood, unable to see, I spoke to you and gave you a purpose and a promise. Do you remember what I said, Greg? 'You've got to fight. Your family is counting on you to fight for your life and come home to them.' Do you remember the picture I placed vividly in your mind over and over again as you took each agonizing, bloody step back to the boat?"

The message was beginning to sink in. "Yes, I do remember, Lord. It was my wife, my sons, and my little girl waving at me and saying, 'Come home, Daddy, please.'"

"I was there for you, Greg, through it all. I never left your side, as I have never left your side from the moment I created you."

Both of us were sobbing now. I put my arms around Jesus and pulled him close to my chest. It was as though our hearts were molded together and were communicating in an unwritten and unspoken language. He didn't need to try to convince me any more. I finally understood that the Lord truly was there for me and had saved my life in many miraculous ways that day. As I sat in my hospital bed, even though I was still enduring intense physical pain, I felt more joy than I had in my entire life.

I wanted this moment with the Lord to go on forever. I squeezed with all my might, hoping our hug would never end. Yet something suddenly felt different. I raised my head.

Once again, I was surprised and confused. Jesus was no longer there. Gripped tightly in my arms was a white hospital pillow. The top of the pillow was soaked with tears.

In disbelief, I let the pillow drop to my lap. Imprinted on the pillowcase was the same bloodstain I'd seen on the back of my dad's shirt.

22

WHAT MATTERS

*See what kind of love the Father has given to us, that we should
be called children of God; and so we are.*
—1 JOHN 3:1 ESV

I pressed my face against the cold glass of the passenger window of Matt's Ford F-250 and stared as millions of acres of green forest raced by. Over the last few hours, my brother and I had barely spoken a word to each other. When we'd traveled this road last, we were so excited, anticipating our greatest adventure ever. Much had changed.

The day after my surgery, I had faced a bucketful of media requests. Matt and I did an interview on FaceTime with a Dallas news team. Then I was able to make calls to family and friends. The staff at Central Peninsula Hospital had treated Matt and me like honored guests. Besides setting up a bed for my brother, they brought him meals and even sectioned off a spot in the parking lot within view of my room for his truck and boat. My surgeon, meanwhile, called Rhea and eased her worries by filling her in on the details. I'd endured six and a half hours of surgery and more than three hundred stitches and staples, and could look forward to future appointments with plastic surgeons, but I was going to live. After three days in the hospital, I'd been released that morning.

We were headed for Matt's home in Wasilla. By the time we picked up antibiotics and pain medication in Soldotna, the sun was already sinking low over the Kenai Peninsula. It was amazing how quickly urban sprawl reverted back to wilderness. As Matt drove, my eyes searched behind every passing rock and tree for the slightest movement of brown fur. If this truck broke down, I was not getting out.

I glanced at Matt and wondered what he was thinking. I was sure that, like me, he'd been going over every detail of the grizzly attack in his mind. I detected sadness in his eyes. I suspected he blamed himself, at least partially, for what had happened.

I hadn't seen much of Matt during my recovery in the hospital. It turned out that the U.S. Fish and Wildlife Service and Alaska state troopers take it pretty seriously when a hunter is mauled by a grizzly bear. They had a lot of questions for my brother. Every year, hunters with little experience and no hunting guide show up in Alaska unprepared and get themselves into trouble. The investigators concluded, however, that the Matthews brothers had known what they were doing and indeed come prepared for anything.

Matt and the two Fish and Wildlife agents agreed it was unlikely the grizzly had survived our encounter. The agents wanted to find that bear. Matt agreed to lead them to the area. He drew a map and predicted where she'd be. The next day, not a hundred yards from the point of the attack and exactly where Matt had anticipated, they came across the massive sow. One of the agents examined her and took measurements.

When the agent pulled back the bear's lips, he found something odd. The lower left fang hung by a sliver of flesh and was folded flat.

On the opposite side, the lower jaw had been split in half. Based on Matt's descriptions, the agents decided the lone possible explanation was that the single round I'd fired during the bear's charge had caused the damage.

The agent allowed the lip to fall back and looked up at Matt. "The only reason your brother is alive," he said, "is that this bear did not have full use of its jaw. If it had, we'd be out here on a body recovery."

My brother just smiled. "A miracle shot is what that was," he said. "We saw a lot of miracles that day."

The agent pulled out a knife and explained that he was required to remove the grizzly's head and paws for further research and DNA testing. It inspired Matt to make an unusual request.

"It would mean a lot to me," he said, "if I could take off the head and paws of the grizzly who nearly robbed me of my brother."

The agent hesitated for only a moment. "Have at it."

I'm sure my screams still echoed in Matt's head as he went to work. Though I know he felt a measure of sorrow over the death of this mighty monarch of the wilderness, I also know he would have done it all again to save the life of his older sibling.

SIX HOURS AFTER WE'D LEFT the hospital, Matt backed the Alumaweld boat into his driveway and I stepped gingerly out of the truck. It was good to be here. I looked forward to being with Matt's family, to Melinda's cooking, to lying in a bed without monitors beeping in my ear and nurses waking me up to check on me.

Most of all, though, I looked forward to seeing Dad.

On the phone the day before, I'd told Dad that Matt and I would be arriving at my brother's house early the next evening. He was excited to hear it, because Melinda was picking him up that afternoon at the Anchorage airport. I could hear the concern, even fear, in his voice. He wasn't going to rest until he confirmed in person that his oldest son was all right. He ended our call by saying, "Greg, I love you, I'm extremely happy to hear you're okay, and I'll be waiting for you in Wasilla."

Just knowing that Dad was flying up gave me a powerful sense of peace. I'd been beaten up physically and emotionally. My body had more holes in it than a piece of Swiss cheese, and the pain remained intense. On the outside, I looked like a mess. On the inside, I felt like a scared little boy, desperate to be held by his daddy and told everything would be fine.

What Dad didn't know—what no one knew—was what I'd experienced in the darkness of my hospital room after the surgery.

I hadn't said a word about it, partly because I'm a private person and mostly because I figured no one would believe me anyway. I wasn't quite sure I believed it myself. Dad, or some spiritual manifestation of him, had visited me in my room . . . and then I'd come face-to-face with the Lord? I knew some people—maybe most people—would say it was a hallucination, a product of trauma, drugs, and exhaustion. But that sure wasn't what it felt like. Words did not exist to adequately explain it.

Whether the Lord had been physically present or not, I knew one thing for certain: he had spoken to me. I finally understood, all the way down in the depths of my soul, that he had been with me throughout the grizzly attack, just when I needed him. That in fact he'd been with me every day of my life.

I wasn't hungry when I walked in the front door of Matt's house, but the inviting aroma of Melinda's incredible cooking—she was making a moose roast with mashed potatoes and green beans—immediately made me feel at home. Then I saw Dad.

Dad was no longer the physically intimidating protector he'd been when I was growing up. His shoulders were a bit more stooped, and the fatigue and worry lines around his eyes were a bit more pronounced. Even so, when he smiled, hurried toward me, and wrapped me in a giant hug, it was one of the most secure feelings I'd ever known. He could barely speak, but when he managed to whisper, "I thought I'd lost you, son," it melted my heart.

Dad was here. Everything was going to be all right.

The next three days included retellings of our adventure and catching up with family, as well as figuring out how to manage my pain and early recovery. Matt's family took turns changing my bandages and deep-swabbing puncture wounds. Even my nephew Gareth wanted to help Uncle Greg, so I allowed him to change the bandages on some of the worst wounds.

One afternoon, everyone gathered around my designated resting spot on the couch and handed me a series of wrapped presents. I opened up a coffee mug that sported the slogan "Don't Feed the Bears," as well as oversized grizzly fur slippers with fake claws and a T-shirt displaying the statement "America's First Homeland Security" and a picture of two grizzly bears. Even though portions of my face had no feeling, I couldn't help laughing. But for the majority of those days, I slept.

The night before Dad and I were scheduled to fly back to Texas, Matt and I went into the garage to go through our combined hunting gear so we could get mine packed. We'd already discovered a plug of flesh from the grizzly's throat in the barrel of my rifle. Now every smell that reminded me of the attack—and there were a lot of them— made me sick to my stomach. I finally told Matt, "I'm done. Just stuff everything in a box. I don't care." I turned and walked back into the house.

The next morning, from the moment we stepped through the doors of the Anchorage airport, I felt like my dad's little boy again. Dad took care of everything. He worked his magic at the counter to get us an early boarding due to my injury. He held our tickets. He researched where we would need to go through security and what direction to take to find our gate. He even found someone to haul our bags and get us checked in. Each time someone helped us, he slipped his hand into his pocket and thanked them with a little cash.

A flight attendant sat us in the front row of first class. I had so much legroom that I felt guilty as people walked by and headed to the back of the plane. Before everyone was seated and the front door secured, the flight attendant placed a hot cup of coffee in my hand and took my order for breakfast. This was going to be a nice flight and I owed it all to Dad. I thanked God that he was there for me.

When I leaned back into the comfort of my leather seat and thought about it, I realized that he'd always been there for me. Every time I'd faced tough situations—including those of my own making—Dad had been on the scene, ready to discipline or encourage me, depending on what I needed most. He'd made mistakes like any father, but he'd always given his best, walked alongside me, and supported me.

Reality hit me then like a blow from a hammer: Dad *loved* me, without any reservations or conditions. He always had. It didn't matter what I accomplished in my career or how I performed. He just loved me.

And so did God.

For most of my life, ever since Dad drove his Chevy Malibu out of our driveway when I was eight, I'd believed 100 percent in the lies I'd been telling myself. I believed that I wasn't good enough, that I'd disappointed my dad and God and made them angry at me, that I'd made unforgivable mistakes, that I had to earn the right to be loved and seen as worthy, that the only person I could count on was myself. It took a devastating attack of a wild grizzly bear for me to finally be awakened to the truth.

I'd always relied on myself to overcome any crisis. I had trained myself to be ready for anything so I could play "the man" and use my skills and experience to save the day. And for most of my life, that approach had worked. But when that bear had me pinned on the ground, I was helpless. No amount of training could change the reality of my situation. I had nothing left to fight with. I had no ability to rescue myself or control the outcome. I was at God's mercy.

Which was exactly where I needed to be for the Lord to do his work.

Incredibly, God had shown up in his perfect timing to not only save my life but permanently heal my heart. When a doctor performs surgery, he often inflicts pain and tissue damage to correct a life-threatening injury. He will cut through healthy tissue to reach the wound. If he doesn't, the patient dies.

I hadn't known it, but I had desperately needed heart surgery—not the type performed by someone with the title of "M.D." following their name, but a divine surgery of the heart that could be performed only by God himself. The surgery was to remove a malignancy that had long ago spread to every part of my mind and body, blocking my ability to love myself or trust the love of a father. For years I'd tortured myself, believing that I was responsible for my parents' divorce and that my father and God—along with everyone else I cared about—would love me only if I performed well enough to earn that love. That lie had poisoned each of my relationships, preventing me from enjoying the blessing of the people the Lord had brought into my life. No matter how perfect I tried to be, it was never enough. I had no rest and knew no peace. Instead, my soul knew only exhaustion from the constant effort of trying to prove myself to each of them.

I realized that now, for the first time in forty years, the malignancy that had plagued my body and soul was gone. I was healthy. I was free. God loved me completely, without reservation, just the way I was.

Over the last few days, almost everything I'd believed had been flipped. God had allowed me to slip within a bear's whisker of death, then turned the tables. More important, he'd shown me *why* he'd allowed me to go through all that trauma. I realized, to my surprise, that I was actually feeling grateful for the grizzly attack. Even crazier, I realized I would go through the horror and pain all over again for another minute in the arms of Jesus. That was where I wanted to be and where I belonged. I could now see that even though I'd been relentless in judging myself unworthy, and even though the grizzly had been relentless in trying to take my life, the love of my dad and my God was even more unyielding. Wild, relentless love had won out.

I glanced at Dad in the airline seat next to me. He was halfway through a movie and had fallen asleep. The worry and energy he'd expended on me had finally caught up with him. I watched his chest rise and fall and again thanked God for my father. Outside the window, sunshine filtered through puffy clouds of white as we winged away from the land of the midnight sun toward home.

Though I'd spent just two weeks in Alaska, it felt as if a very long chapter in my life was coming to a close. I was leaving with new eyes. No longer would they strain to look over the horizon for the next new passion, adventure, or goal to establish my value. Now the only things that mattered were living in relationship with God and my family and fulfilling the Lord's plans for me. I was called to be a loving son, husband, and father. My world had gotten a lot smaller and my vision was suddenly much clearer.

DESPITE THE AMAZING CARE I'D been given by the Central Peninsula staff and the incredible grace God had shown me, I developed a secret fear while recovering at the hospital. It sounds a bit shallow, but it was all about my face.

Based on the throbbing pain I felt in my neck, head, and face, I was certain that my injuries were grotesque. I imagined deep scars that made my previous features unrecognizable. Even worse, I feared that my nine-year-old daughter would be unable to look at me. Casey and Ben could handle it. I knew Rhea loved me to the moon and she'd find a way to cope with a disfigured husband. But I was tortured by the idea that Ciara would see me as a monster.

I was too afraid of what I might see to even glance at a mirror.

My fears were magnified when I called Rhea from my bed on my third day in the hospital. I reassured her that I was okay and said nothing about my worry that I'd become the Phantom of the Opera. There was an ominous pause in our conversation.

"Please don't take this the wrong way," Rhea said. "You know how much Ciara loves you. She said she doesn't want to come to the airport and see you all cut up. She said she would cry too much."

I got off the phone as quick as I could. As far as I was concerned, my nightmare had just been confirmed. I pulled the bedcovers over my head and fought the urge to scream. At the time, I was still processing the astonishing visitation from God. Meanwhile, the familiar lies and feelings of devastating emotional pain pounded at the walls of my mind. To make matters worse, for the last three days I'd refused to look in the bathroom mirror for fear of what would look back at me.

After a few minutes, however—through either a nudge from the Lord or simply despair—I realized I had to confront the truth. My feet met the cold tile floor leading to the bathroom. With my eyes closed and my body shaking, I stepped in front of the mirror.

I opened my eyes. My face was swollen and marred by a number of lacerations and puncture holes. My lip had been torn through and a chunk of flesh was missing from the bottom of my chin. Two lacerations marked by blue stitches ran down the front of my forehead. More stitches closed the holes where the bear's fangs had gone through my temple and through my cheek and into my jawbone. Two dozen staples attached my scalp to my skull.

It wasn't pretty. And yet, it did still look like me. After a half hour of cleanup with a moist washrag, I was even more recognizable. I was just presentable enough to think my daughter might be able to handle it.

I called Rhea using FaceTime on my cell phone. "Babe," I said, "I really need you to look at my face and tell me if it's too scary for Ciara to see." I held the phone out so Rhea could see everything.

I hadn't realized Ciara was sitting next to Rhea. My wife turned to our daughter. "Ciara, Daddy's on the phone. He's wondering if you want to talk to him."

I heard my daughter's answer: "Sure."

Ciara took the phone and nearly pressed her nose to the screen, her eyes darting to all corners of the phone, trying to take it all in. She shifted her gaze to the upper right corner of the phone and my forehead, then scanned down until she was looking at my chin. Next she examined the holes in my face. She had no idea how much this meant to me. I held my breath and waited.

After what seemed an eternity, Ciara finally leaned back and pronounced her verdict: "Oh, Daddy," she said, "you don't look that bad. I'll come see you at the airport."

I teared up at the memory as we started our descent into Dallas/ Fort Worth. My healing from the grizzly mauling had begun with my brother's caregiving at the attack site and continued with the nurturing and skillful treatment by the hospital staff and, of course, the Lord's intervention, and my dad's bringing me home. But true healing could not begin until I was again surrounded by my family. I needed to hear their voices and feel their touch. In more ways than one, they had saved my life.

When we landed, I was so eager to see them that I was nearly sick to my stomach. I'm sure Dad was talking to me as we made our way to the baggage claim, but his words barely registered. My heart and mind were focused on one thing. I was supposed to walk slowly, but my pace quickened as we approached the plate-glass windows and doors leading to the outside world. Eagerly, I scanned the crowd that waited for new arrivals.

Then I saw them. Ciara spotted me at the same moment I saw her. She started screaming and jumping up and down, a "Welcome Home" sign in her hands. Ben thrust his own sign high into the air to make sure I saw it. Rhea was crying.

I couldn't hold back any longer. I sprinted toward them, my own tears flowing. Ciara threw her sign to the ground and bolted my way, with Ben right behind. I dropped to my knees, threw down my bags, and opened my arms. My kids wrapped their arms around my neck so tight that I thought they were permanently attached. Rhea soon completed the circle by enfolding us in her arms. "Thank you, God," she whispered, "for bringing Greg home."

Other arriving passengers gave us a wide berth as they headed toward the exits. I'm sure we were a spectacle. I couldn't have cared less. I was back where I belonged.

23

NEW LIFE

Therefore, if anyone is in Christ, he is a new creation; the old has gone, the new has come!
—2 CORINTHIANS 5:17 NIV

On my first morning back home, I showered and slipped on shorts and a sweatshirt. As usual, Rhea was already up and in the kitchen. I made my way down the hallway and past one of my favorite images, a lithograph on our living room wall that portrayed Jesus guiding the hands of a surgeon in the middle of an operation. I stopped at the breakfast bar facing the kitchen and watched Rhea, wearing her white bathrobe, make coffee. It was a routine we'd performed a thousand times before.

Then she handed me my coffee in my new "Don't Feed the Bears" mug. As much as this morning seemed the same as so many others . . . it wasn't. I'd assumed a new perspective on life. Now I had to figure out how to apply it.

It wasn't long before I faced my first opportunity. Rhea informed me that people in our neighborhood, some that we didn't even know, had signed up to bring us meals. It had started before I got home and was scheduled to continue for at least the next month. The people of Texas are amazing.

I'd never had to rely on others like this. It was a tough pill to swallow. When it came to my family—or just about anything else—I considered it a sign of weakness to depend on someone else. It meant I wasn't doing my job as a husband and father.

At least, that was how I used to think. If I'd learned anything from the grizzly attack, however, it was that I didn't always have to prove myself or take on every challenge alone. As strange and uncomfortable as it felt, it was actually okay to ask for help. When I thought more about it, I realized that Rhea had her hands full serving as my caretaker while also being mom for the kids. Not only that, but since she was mostly housebound because of my injuries, she was missing out on her usual social interaction. She needed people to talk to. I decided the meal plan wasn't such a bad idea.

I must have needed more practice with that lesson, because it kept coming back. The news media had camped out in front of our house the day after the grizzly attack. Rhea had already dodged them for a few hours that day and asked Ben to sneak in and out through the alley behind our house until she figured out what to tell them. Starting about ten on my first morning at home and continuing for the rest of the day, our phones rang nonstop. *Good Morning America*, National Public Radio, the British newspaper the *Guardian*, and just about every local and regional news outlet wanted to interview me. I was suddenly a reluctant celebrity.

Rhea knew I was overwhelmed physically and emotionally, and that I wasn't in a good state to handle the media. She asked if I could get someone to help us map out a strategy for who to give interviews to and what to say. Of course it bothered me that she had to deal with pressure from TV and print reporters, especially since I was the cause of it. And I realized I was far from at my best. Yet I hesitated to ask for assistance. The instinct to take care of everything on my own was strong.

Once again, however, I acknowledged that this was a situation where I didn't need to prove myself to anyone. Plus, I knew just who to call. Bryan was a good friend, paramedic, and firefighter who'd had training on how to address the media at the scene of an emergency. He coordinated my interviews, prepared me ahead of time, and did a fantastic job of managing the situation. Initially, I also asked Bryan to change my bandages, which he gladly did.

I was thankful for Bryan's presence, but this new approach to life was going to take some getting used to.

Then there was my would-be nurse, my daughter. I had a wound kit that included a thin bamboo swab with cotton on the end. The doctor's orders were to force that swab into the holes in my arms and leg, clean and irrigate the area, and then pack it with gauze—twice or three times a day. No question, it was gross. But when Ciara saw me working on it, she came over and said, "Dad, can I help you with that?"

My first thought had always been to protect my family's eyes and hearts from anything uncomfortable or painful. I did not want my daughter looking at my wounds. Yet I understood that Ciara was one of the reasons I'd even survived the grizzly attack. Would I be stealing something important from her if I refused to let her participate in my recovery as well? Maybe this was an opportunity for me to give up some control and allow our relationship to grow.

The next time my wounds needed cleaning, I set everything up on a table, showed Ciara what to do, and let her go to it. "Does that hurt, Daddy?" she asked. "Should I go deeper?" She gave it her very best. For the next week, Ciara was in charge of my wound kit. During those days we bonded like we never had before.

More than anything, however, what stuck out the most as truly different in my new life was the first few moments of each day. I had always gotten up early and was quick to focus on my priorities for the day. I had goals to achieve, after all.

Now, however, I was in no hurry to leave the bed. I gazed at our ceiling fan and waited for slivers of yellow and orange sun rays to slip over the sill of the bay window. Work was still important, but it could wait a few minutes—I was loved even if I didn't conquer the world that day. I listened to myself breathe and let my mind wander. Often, I returned to the same amazing thought, that I was honestly thankful for the grizzly attack.

It was both strange and wonderful. "Joy" and "peace" weren't just nice words you'd read on a Christmas card. They defined my whole being in those moments.

Not that all my problems had suddenly been solved. I experienced a measure of post-traumatic stress and preferred to be alone for hours at a time. I never had any nightmares, but images of the attack played in my mind like a recurring TV commercial. So many people asked about what had happened and wanted to hear the story. Yet each time I talked about being mauled, I could see in the eyes of my listeners that they really had no idea what it was like. I grew more and more frustrated with each retelling. When I was a firefighter and something traumatic happened on the job, invariably several of us went through it together and could talk about it afterward. This time, I sensed that no one truly understood. I started feeling as if I were going to explode.

My release turned out to be writing. Less than two weeks after my homecoming, I began typing out the events in Alaska and what I thought about them. Recording my feelings was more cathartic than I could have imagined.

I was also encouraged by the support of well-wishers. Late one night, for example, I took a call from Chris, one of the Fish and Wildlife agents who'd worked with Matt. It wasn't anything official, just one man reaching out to another and asking if there was anything he could do. It was a gesture I deeply appreciated.

Of all the encouraging calls and messages I received, however, the most meaningful arrived about a week after I returned home. Dad had stayed with us an extra four days after escorting me back. He wanted to make sure that I was going to be fine. About four days after he left, he sent an email.

"I've been up all night," he wrote. "I don't know what I would have done if I had lost you. I know I came so very close to losing you out there. I just want you to know that I love you very much and that I couldn't be more proud of you."

Over the years, my dad had changed. He'd learned to move past the persona of the stoic alpha male and let out more of his compassion and feelings. He'd gone out of his way to establish a relationship with all three of my kids. No conversation ended without Dad telling each of them that he loved them. He enjoyed giving the kids gifts, handing them cash as a reward for good grades, and taking them to the movies. He never said so, but I think he was trying to make up for lost opportunities. I could definitely relate to the idea of resetting your compass heading.

Despite his new attitude, though, that email was an astonishing thing for him to write. It revealed a level of affection I'd never seen before. To me, it was confirmation of my awakening in the wilderness and in that hospital bed—that my dad really had always loved me. The divorce and his departure were not because of anything I'd done. He was a man trying his best to play the hand he'd been dealt, just as I was.

Perhaps more important, I realized that if Dad had known about the darkness that would engulf me after he drove away, he never would have left.

It took me two days to email back, because I wanted to get the words right. I finally wrote, "Hey Dad, thank you so much for the email you sent. It just completes everything that the Lord had begun and worked through that day. I'll never forget you dropping everything and being there at Matt's house when I arrived, never leaving my side, getting me home, and taking care of my family. I'll always keep your email. Thank you for speaking to me from your heart."

I had spent so many years believing so many lies. It should never have taken being clutched in the jaws of a grizzly for me to finally understand what was important in life. Now, however, I wouldn't trade my tangle with that bear for anything in the world. It was allowing me to live with a new perspective and a peace I'd never known. And it had blessed my family. I was glad to have a chance to make up for lost time.

AS THE WEEKS AND THEN months of my recovery stretched on, a strange thing happened. Rhea's friends came to visit her at the house and inevitably asked me about the bear attack. After I related what had happened—by now I felt less stressed about sharing the details— their universal response was "You've got to tell that story to my husband."

So I did. My male audiences were nearly always riveted. I found myself saying, "I don't know what you believe, but I can't tell this story without sharing about the miracles that God did, the ways he interceded and changed me." I talked about standing at the lip of the abyss, with death calling for me, and coming to realize that instead of career achievements it was relationships that mattered.

My story seemed to have an impact. Unexpectedly, talking about it resonated in a new way with me. I realized that many men had wounds that created a distance between them and their wives and kids. I sensed that the Lord wanted me to keep sharing about what had happened to me and how we get disconnected from what is most important.

I was particularly encouraged when Gene, a local pastor and author, took time out of his busy schedule to listen to my story. By this time I was already thinking in terms of reaching men on a bigger scale. Gene's enthusiasm confirmed to me that I was on the right track. Whether it was speaking opportunities, a book, or a ministry, I'd found a new channel for my passion for making a difference—one where my sense of value didn't depend on the outcome.

I was done with collecting glittering trophies that in truth were more like trash. Now I was after treasure. For the rest of my days, I would cherish the people I loved. I was grateful for them beyond words—and for a daddy in heaven who'd been there for me through it all, and was there for me still.

LIVE LIKE YOU WERE DYING

Most men long for adventure and conquest. We have written into our DNA a warrior spirit, a passion to achieve. What I didn't understand for so many years, what I believe many men are searching to discover, is that the primary purpose for this deep-seated desire has nothing to do with careers, making money, or hobbies. The purpose of our passion is to pursue meaningful relationships with God and our families.

Are you, like me, a man who's been shooting his arrows at the wrong target? Can you relate to the idea of dedicating yourself to being the best at whatever you do while having a nagging suspicion that what you reserve for God and your wife and children is "leftovers"?

Men, our families need us. For so long, pleas for attention from our wives, daughters, and sons have fallen on deaf ears. They are desperate to have their cries heard. I'm sure if Rhea and my kids were given the option, they would trade away all my achievements for more time spent in my arms. Your wife and kids want to know that they come before all other things. Even though they would never ask, they need to know that you would lay it all down for them.

If you're a man reading this book, I hope it has inspired you to reorder your life and make relationships your priority. It doesn't mean walking away from other pursuits you enjoy and find meaningful. It simply means diving into what you were designed to do and watching it change everything. If you're a wife, girlfriend, daughter, or other female relative reading this book, I hope you will use it as a tool for reaching out to the men you love and helping them discover what it took me so long to see.

Several years ago, country singer Tim McGraw released a song called "Live Like You Were Dying." Those simple words define who I am today. As crazy as it sounds, I wish that every man alive could stare into the face of death and be given one last shot at getting it right.

On a business trip a while back, I visited Arlington National Cemetery near Washington, D.C., the final resting place for more than four hundred thousand of our nation's military heroes. The view is stirring—endless rows of white crosses and marble headstones aligned on a sea of green grass. In my time there, I did not locate a single inscription that described the fallen service member as a great pilot, sailor, or soldier, or as someone who fought the toughest battles or who built a successful business. No, the engravings on those headstones spoke of relationships. Most concluded with the statement "He was a loving husband" or "He was a loving father," or a combination of both.

If you died today, how would your headstone read? If you don't like the answer, it's not too late to write a new one. You—and your family—will be eternally grateful.

ACKNOWLEDGMENTS

The writing of this book would have never happened had not my brother, Matt, and the Lord Jesus Christ intervened to save my life. For a man to go head-to-head with a massive grizzly is not for the faint of heart. Thank you, Matt! There is no doubt that when I looked into the eyes of death, one reason above all others inspired my fight to survive: the desire to see my family again. Thank you Rhea, Casey, and Benjamin for your never-ending love and for praying me past the moments I thought it was all over. I felt every prayer you lifted. To my eleven-year-old daughter, Ciara: God used you in a special way. When I couldn't go on, it was your voice I heard telling me to "Fight, Daddy." Thank you, honey.

Dad, because of you I had the tenacity to fight and the common sense to overcome the obstacles that stood in the way of me surviving. There is no way to tell the world how much I love you except to say, "When I grow up, I want to be just like you, Dad." To my best friend, thanks for being there.

A deep, heartfelt thank-you goes out to the Central Peninsula Hospital staff and flight crew; Agent Chris Johnson of the U.S. Fish and Wildlife Service; Jeff Selinger, wildlife biologist; and the rest of the first responders who laid their lives on the line to help rescue my brother and me. Having spent over twenty years as a firefighter and emergency manager, I was impressed by the level of response.

Last, but certainly not least, I would like to extend sincere thanks to those who made it possible to bring my story to print. None of this would have happened without the work and passion of my editor, Beth Adams; literary agent Michael Palgon, who believed in me; and the gifting's of writer-editor Jim Lund. To my dear friend Ted Nulty, thank you for inspiring me to write my story. And finally, thank you Ryan Utecht for listening to God and securing me the opportunity to be published.

ABOUT THE AUTHORS

Greg Matthews, driven by a passion to help those who cannot help themselves, has dedicated most of his life to defending our nation and safeguarding the lives of others. After serving in the U.S. Air Force during the Desert Storm and Desert Shield wars, Greg's roles over the next twenty-seven years included firefighter, hazardous materials technician, emergency medical technician, special operations rescue technician, rescue helicopter pilot, fugitive recovery agent, and international consultant on emergency management and security risk management. He designed and executed a national rescue and emergency service program in the remote jungles of Uganda and conducted security assessments that helped protect that nation's citizens from terrorists. In the aftermath of the 9/11 attacks, he flew to New York to search for survivors at Ground Zero. He has been a homeland security manager for the City of San Diego Office of Homeland Security and regional antiterrorism officer for Navy Region Southwest Headquarters, where he was responsible for protecting the largest fleet of U.S naval war assets on the West Coast. Greg currently serves as the U.S. Army Corps of Engineers (USACE) Southwestern Division antiterrorism officer, protecting the nation's dams, hydropower generation plants, and navigation locks.

Greg is committed to loving the Lord and his family, developing deep spiritual and human relationships, and sharing his message that men and their search for manhood are defined by the quality of their relationships. He is the founder of Chase What Matters ministry (www.chasewhatmatters.today), which is a ministry devoted to inspiring men to discover and live out their purpose, starting with an intimate relationship with God and family. Chase What Matters stands on the core principle that true masculinity is defined by the quality of a man's heart, his connection to the Lord, his wife, his children, and other family and friends.

Greg lives in Plano, Texas, with his wife of seventeen years, Rhea, sons Casey and Benjamin, and daughter, Ciara. The Matthews family attends Chase Oaks Church in Plano and spends much of its time watching the kids play baseball and softball.

James Lund is an award-winning collaborator and editor, and the coauthor of *A Dangerous Faith* and *Danger Calling*. He has worked with bestselling authors and public figures such as George Foreman, Kathy Ireland, Max Lucado, Randy Alcorn, Jim Daly, and NFL Hall of Famers Tim Brown and Bruce Matthews. Book sales from Jim's projects exceed three million copies; three of his projects earned the ECPA Gold Medallion Book Award. Visit his website at www.jameslundbooks.com.